Annabel Karmel's
Complete Party Planner

Annabel Karmel's
Complete Party Planner

Over 120 delicious recipes
and party ideas for every occasion

EBURY PRESS
LONDON

To my children Nicholas, Lara and Scarlett who uncomplainingly ate their way through all the birthday cakes, jellies and chocolate biscuits in this book yet surprisingly still managed to demolish all the left-over sweets from the photo shoots.

First published in Great Britain in 2000

7 9 10 8

Text copyright © Annabel Karmel 2000

Photographs (with the exception of those listed on page 191) copyright © Daniel Pangbourne 2000

The right of Annabel Karmel to be identified as the author of this work has been asserted by her in accordance with the Copyright, Designs and Patents Act, 1988.

First published by Ebury Press

Random House · 20 Vauxhall Bridge Road · London SW1V 2SA

Random House Australia (Pty) Limited

20 Alfred Street, Milsons Point · Sydney · New South Wales 2061 · Australia

Random House New Zealand Limited

18 Poland Road · Glenfield · Auckland 10 · New Zealand

Random House South Africa (Pty) Limited

Endulini · 5a Jubilee Road · Parktown 2193 · South Africa

Random House Canada

1265 Aerowood Drive · Mississauga · Ontario L4W 1B9

www.randomhouse.co.uk

A CIP catalogue for this book is available from the British Library

0 09 187526 9
9780091875268 (from January 2007)

Designed by Lovelock & Co. · Editor Emma Callery · Home economist Sarah Lewis · Stylist Tessa Evelegh

Colour Reproduction by Colorlito, Milan

Printed and bound in Singapore by Tien Wah Press

Papers used by Ebury Press are natural recyclable products made from wood grown in sustainable forests.

Contents

Introduction

This is a book for everyone who has something to celebrate, and my aim is to make sure that your child's party goes with a swing. Whether it is a first birthday celebration or you are looking for new ideas and inspiration to come up with something truly memorable after many years of organising children's parties, there is something in this book for you. As a mother of three children I have learnt a lot from my own successes and failures. I remember my daughter showing the first signs of chicken pox and coming out in angry red spots just as her friends were arriving for a fireworks party. Or there was the ill-fated disco party I organised where none of the children wanted to dance and my son's sports party in the pouring rain where it was so muddy it took some skill just to remain upright. Yet sometimes the unexpected can make the day and I overheard one boy tell his dad as he was leaving that he wanted a sports party on his birthday but only if it was raining. It turned out that the boys had more fun sliding around and getting caked in mud than if the sun had been shining!

Parental involvement means far more to your child than spending money on a lavish party. The smile on his or her face mirrors the love you show for your child. Be a part of their fun, don't sit on the sidelines, join in with their growing up – it's such fun. One of the most successful parties I gave my son was a

football party and the highlight was inviting all the dads to play a game of football at the end against the boys. Despite the dads not having played football in at least 20 years, I've never seen a more competitive bunch. Needless to say, the boys loved every minute of it, but I think a lot of the dads suffered later on in the day!

Forward planning and organisation is the secret to success and party preparation is all part of the fun. Once your child is old enough he or she will enjoy being involved in things like helping to make the party invitations, choosing the games or helping prepare the food and this book is packed full of fun activities for you to share with your child.

An approaching birthday is the biggest event in a child's life and although the charm for us wears off around the age of 35, for children they look forward all year, counting the weeks to the special day with feverish excitement. Active participation is definitely a key to success. For my oldest daughter I organised a cooking party where – horror of horrors – no food was prepared in advance and it was up to the children to make their own tea. They had enormous fun rolling out dough, cutting out cookies and making milkshakes. Yes, it was messy and you needed a team of willing helpers but boy was it worth it to see their little faces beaming with pride at their new-found culinary skills. For

KEY FOR SYMBOLS
easy for children to help
N contains nuts
❄ suitable for freezing

my youngest daughter I organised a beauty and jewellery making party where the girls' faces and hair were made up, their nails painted and before and after pictures taken. In between, the budding supermodels also had the chance to make jewellery and play party games.

From the original and fun invitation that sets the mood to the last crumb of the novelty birthday cake, I hope that this book will help ensure that your child's party is truly memorable.

Party Planning

Planning your Party

I always think that there is something quite personal about having a party at home, but it does involve quite a lot of organising. You will probably need to move some of the furniture so there is enough room for the children to play games and, if there are a lot of children, you may need to hire in tables and chairs for the tea. But if the thought of a whole bunch of excited kids running amok in your house fills you with dread, the answer might be to hold your party somewhere else.

Think about where you would like to hold the party in plenty of time as some venues may need to be booked months in advance. Some ideas for possible venues include a local church hall, a school hall, an indoor gymnasium or the local park. Other venues such as a skating rink, swimming pool, football pitch, museum (some museums even allow children to have a sleepover), the zoo, theme park, the circus, the theatre or cinema, a waterslide park or a junior go-kart track, will determine the theme of the party.

Involving your Child

Whatever you choose to do, involve your child in the decision making and party preparation. Birthday parties are a big event in a child's life and it is really important that your child be included in this way. There are many things that your child can

TIP

For little children of two and under, invite parents along as well. Toddlers need more attention than one or two adults can give. At this age they won't need organised games, so have lots of toys for them to play with.

be involved in, perhaps drawing a picture for the invitations, which you can then photocopy, or choosing the kind of games to be played. Sharing the party planning with you will be very exciting for your child and give them an enormous sense of importance – quite right and proper for their big day after all.

Entertainment

Children's party entertainers tend to be very popular but they are expensive and the good ones will need to be booked well in advance. Of course, it makes life much easier to let the entertainer organise the entertainment for you, but in my experience, nothing will delight your child more than your efforts and the time you put in to make sure the party goes with a swing. There are such a fantastic variety of party games for all ages and I find that children want to take part rather than be spectators. Don't make the party too long, 2 to 2½ hours is just about right.

Tip

If planning an outdoor party, do not assume the weather will be good, have an alternative indoor venue that is close by.

The Party Countdown

8 weeks ahead

Book the venue and entertainer (if appropriate).

4 weeks ahead

Decide on how many children you want to invite and make a guest list with the help of your child.

Decide on the theme or entertainment.

Make and send invitations.

Organise fancy dress (if appropriate).

Decide on your helpers, they may be parents, relatives or friends.

Hire tables and chairs (if necessary).

1 week ahead

Buy paper plates, cups, napkins, balloons, candles, cake board.

Buy decorations, like banners and streamers.

Plan the games, buy any special props and make a list.

Choose the music: each age group has their favourite music from nursery rhymes for very young children to the latest pop songs for older children.

Buy non-perishable ingredients for the food.

Buy going-home presents (if necessary) and prizes and wrap them.

Make a list of food for the party. Spread the food preparation over several days and make any party food that you want to freeze in the week before the party.

2 days ahead

Call any RSVPs who have not responded.

Draw up the final guest list.

Shop for the remaining food for the party.

Baking day: bake the birthday cake and make the cakes and biscuits.

Make up the party bags (if necessary).

Sort out party clothes.

Buy film for camera and make sure you have spare batteries.

Make sure you have candles and matches for the cake.

1 day ahead

Decorate the cake.

Prepare jellies and any other party food that would be fine prepared the day ahead.

Decorate the house and table.

Prepare the games.

Day of the party

Make the fresh party food like sandwiches, fresh fruit, etc. Keep sandwiches fresh by covering them with a damp cloth like a clean tea towel.

Blow up the balloons or buy some helium-filled balloons.

If holding the party at home, decorate the front door with balloons and maybe a banner saying happy birthday.

Put a sign on the loo door and lock rooms that are out of bounds.

Set the table and lay out the food.

Tips

Keep a first aid kit on hand at the party in case of accidents

Do not give children under the age of three peanuts

Making invitations

An original hand-made invitation will set the scene for a very special party. Making your own invitations can be a lot of fun, too, but keep your design quite simple as you will need to make it several times. If possible, get your child involved in helping to make the invitations.

Jigsaw invitation

You will need: bought, hand-drawn and photocopied or computer generated invitations

Write out all the details on the invitations or print them on the computer. Then cut the invitation into lots of pieces like a jigsaw puzzle. Put in a little note to say something like, 'Let's get together' and send to each of the guests.

Baby Photo Invitation

You will need: cute photograph of the birthday girl or boy
as a baby, balloons, permanent black marker pen
Photocopy the baby photo on a colour photocopier and
write on the front something like, 'Guess Who's Having a
Birthday Party!' and add the party details on the back.

Balloon Invitation

Inflate a balloon but do not tie it. Ask someone to hold it for
you and write the party details on the surface of the balloon
using a permanent felt tip pen, then let out the air. Place the
balloon in an envelope with a note instructing the guest to blow
up the balloon.

Party Games

Pick party games that are right for your child's age. They should be challenging but not too difficult. Have some inexpensive prizes on hand for the winners and try to make sure that everyone has a chance to win a prize. The first half hour of a party can be awkward, especially if some of the children don't know each other, so it is good to get them involved right from the start in some games to break the ice. Messy games like the Egyptian Mummy (see page 21) are best reserved for the end of the party.

Icebreakers

Paper Bag Mystery

Props: paper bags, mystery objects, tie

Label paper bags with each letter of your child's name and put objects that start with the corresponding letter into each of the bags and then tie them at the top. The children have to guess what is in each of the bags by feeling the outside of the bag.

The Power of Advertising

Props: old magazines, scissors, pencils and paper

Cut out pictures or photographs advertising products from magazines, but make sure the product is not shown or mentioned. Pin them all over the house before the children arrive. When they take off their coats, give each of the children a piece of paper and a pencil. The children then have to try to write down what the product is. Ten minutes after the last guest has arrived, collect all the lists – whoever has identified the most products is the winner.

Hidden Stars

Prop: packets of small coloured stars

Hide the stars around the room before the party. How well hidden they are will really depend on the children's age. The aim is for the children to find as many pairs of the same coloured stars as they can. This could also be played with mini Smarties.

Hunt the Ping Pong Balls

Props: ping pong balls, permanent black marker pen

Give every guest a ping pong ball with their name on when they arrive and send them off one by one to another room to hide it. When the last guest has hidden the ball it is time for all the guests to start looking for them. The guest whose ball is the last to be found is the winner.

Indoor Party Games

Musical Newspapers

Props: old newspapers

Space out sheets of newspaper on the floor with one less than the number of children. Put on the music and the children can dance around. When the music stops, the children must leap on to a sheet of newspaper and the child who doesn't find one is out. Remove another piece and start again, until there is only one person left. The same game can be played with pillows.

Memory Game

Props: a tray, various objects, pencils and paper

Put a tray of objects in front of the children and they have 2 minutes in which to memorise the items. The older the children are, the more items you can put on the tray. Remove the tray and the children must write down on a piece of paper as many of the objects as they can remember.

Jelly Bean Hunt

Props: jelly beans

Assign a point value to each colour of jelly bean. The highest value going to the colour with the fewest number of beans. Hide the beans in the party room so they are in sight but well camouflaged. Set a time limit, at the end of which the child with the most points is the winner.

Hoop-la

Props: empty milk bottles, six hoops

Arrange a collection of empty milk bottles on bits of paper with a score written on each. Get some hoops or cut out hoops from strong card and give each child six. The children stand behind a line and can throw hoops at the bottles. If they go right over, they score the number of points written on the piece of paper on which they land.

Eat the Chocolate

Props: a very large bar of chocolate, plastic plate, knife and fork, dice, hat, scarf, pair of gloves, sunglasses

The children sit in a circle and they take turns to throw the dice. Anyone who throws a six, leaps up, puts on all the clothes and then has to try and cut and eat as much chocolate as possible until someone else throws a six. Sometimes a six is thrown even before the child manages to get all the clothes on so you have to be quick. The winner is the child who eats the most chocolate.

Jumping Balloon Race

Props: two balloons

Line up two teams at one end of a room behind a line. Give the person at the front of each team a balloon, which they should hold between their knees. On the given signal, the leaders race to the end of the room and back, jumping with the balloon between their knees. The balloon is given to each of the next players in turn and the winner is the team whose last player first arrives behind the line with the balloon. If the balloon floats away, then whoever let it go must return to the start line and begin again.

The Egyptian Mummy
Props: toilet rolls
Divide the children into teams and one 'mummy' must be chosen from each team (they should be about the same size) and given a roll of toilet paper. The mummies then stand facing their teams with their legs together and arms by their sides. On 'Go!', the first in each team runs up to their mummy and starts to bandage with the toilet paper, starting at the feet and working upwards. After 30 about seconds, the second player runs up and takes over and so on. If the paper tears, it must be tucked neatly into the folds before starting again. The winning team is the one that most successfully covers the mummy in a given time. The next prize is for the mummy who can divest him- or herself of the wrappings the quickest.

Bomb Squad
Props: alarm clock with a ticking sound
Have the children leave the room. Wind up the clock and set it for three minutes. Hide it but make sure the ticking sound is still audible. Have the children return to the room and tell them that their job is to listen for the bomb and find it before it goes off in three minutes. As the seconds tick by, the suspense will build up. If the children are quite successful at locating the bomb you can make it more challenging by setting the clock for 2 minutes or even just one.

Siamese Twins

Props: tennis balls

Divide the children into two teams of even numbers and get them to stand at one end of the room. The first and second players hold hands and face each other and a tennis ball is put between their foreheads. They have to run to the far end of the room and back without dropping the ball. If the ball drops they have to go back and start again. When the first couple successfully returns, they place the ball between the second pair's foreheads, and so on until everyone in the team has had a go. If you want the game to last longer, you could allow each pair two goes.

Fishing Game

Props: old newspapers, wool

Cut out fish from newspaper and thread lengths of wool through their heads. Players tie the wool round their waists so that the fish are just trailing on the floor behind them. On 'Go!' everyone has to try and catch each other's fish by stamping on them, but at the same time keeping their own fish intact. The last one to keep his or her fish on the line is the winner.

Blind Man's Buff

Props: a dark scarf to make a good blindfold

One of the guests volunteers to be blindfolded and is then turned around several times until disorientated. The other players move around quietly in a fairly small area and the blindfolded player has to try and catch one of them. It is a good idea to first remove any objects from the room that you think might get broken. Once caught, the player then has to stand still while the blindfolded child feels his or her face and body with his hands and tries to guess who is the captive. If the guess is correct, the two change places and the game starts again.

Paper Fashion Show

Props: newspaper, sticky tape, scissors, string or ribbon and whatever odds and ends you can find like leftover wrapping paper or wallpaper

Divide the children into pairs and put all the props on to a table. One of each couple has to make an outfit for the partner to wear – give them a time limit of about 15 minutes. Then hold a fashion show so that everyone can vote, giving marks out of ten for each outfit. But no one is allowed to vote for their own outfit.

Guess Whose Feet

Props: paper, pen, large sheet

Divide the guests into two teams and send one team out of the room. The other team takes off their shoes and socks and lies down on the floor in a straight row. Drape a sheet over them so that only their feet are sticking out and put a piece of paper with a number on next to each pair of feet. Tell the children to be very quiet and as still as possible and then bring the other team into the room. The members of this team then have to make a list of who they think the feet belong to. When they have chosen, remove the sheet and reveal the children's identities. Repeat with the second team. The team that has the most correct answers is the winner.

Famous People

Make up a chart of anagrams made up of famous people's names. Give each child pencil and paper and see how many names they can work out in a given time.

Pass the Parcel (with a twist)

Props: one large present, various small presents, wrapping paper and newspaper, pen and paper

Choose one big prize and lots of little prizes like sweets, pencils, rubbers, hair ornaments. Also write several forfeits on pieces of paper like 'sing a song' or 'stand on your head'.

First wrap the main prize in newspaper, then continue to wrap in more layers of newspaper and in each layer choose to put either a small prize or forfeit. Arrange the children in a circle, start the music and get them to pass the parcel around the circle. When the music stops the child holding the parcel has to unwrap one layer, enjoying the forfeit or prize accordingly. Continue until someone gets to unwrap the main present. Whoever is controlling the music should make sure that everyone in the circle gets a turn to unwrap the present.

Ambidextrous Skills

Props: pen, paper, pencils, hat

Have the same number of pieces of paper as guests and on each write the name of an object like a chair or a television. Put the pieces of paper in a hat and choose one of the children to take out a piece of paper and then draw the object with the wrong hand. Whoever guesses correctly is next.

Sucking Smarties

Props: straws, Smarties, bowl and plate

Have a pile of Smarties on a plate and an empty bowl. The object of the game is to get as many Smarties as possible into the bowl by sucking them on to the end of the straw and then letting them drop into the bowl. Use a new straw for each competitor and the one to transfer the most Smarties in a set time is the winner.

Outdoor Games

Wheelbarrow Race

This is a fun game for outdoors on a lawn. Everyone chooses a partner. The children take it in turns to be the wheelbarrow and walk on their hands while the other child holds their ankles. For an even more difficult game you can attempt to do this backwards.

Sack Race

Props: black bin liners

Everyone climbs into a 'sack' or black bin liner. On 'Go!' they jump along with both feet in the sack. The first one to cross the finishing line without falling over is the winner.

Spud and Spoon Race

Props: large spoons and potatoes

On 'Go!' the children have to run to the finishing line balancing a potato on a spoon. If the potato falls off they must pick it up with the spoon as fast as possible, but without touching it with their fingers, and begin again.

Crab Race

Line up teams at one end of a garden (or room) and show them how to grasp their ankles and run sideways like a crab. Each member of the team has to go to the far end of the garden and back and then the second member of the team can go and so on. The winning team is the one whose last member gets back to base first. Any children who let go of their ankles or fall over have to start all over again.

Up and Under

Form the teams into lines and space each member about 0.5 metre apart. The child at the back leapfrogs over the one in front, crawls between the legs of the next player, leapfrogs the third and so on. As soon as a player has been jumped over or crawled under she or he has to move back a place. As soon as the first team member has completed the line, the next player has a turn. The first team back in their original position is the winning team.

Dressing-up Race

Props: 2 hats, 2 shirts, 2 pairs of trousers, 2 pairs of sunglasses, 2 pairs of boots

This is a relay race with a difference for two teams. Have a hat, shirt, trousers, sunglasses and boots laid out at equally spaced intervals on the way to the finishing line. The players must run to the clothes and put them on as they come to them, then run to the finishing line, touch it and race back again removing the clothes in reverse order, thereby leaving them in the correct place for the next player. Each player completes the course and the team that finishes first is the winner.

Nature Scavenger Hunt

Make a list of things to find in nature, such as a pine cone, daisy, leaf. Give a copy of the list to each child, set a time limit and the child who manages to gather the most objects or the team with the most objects is the winner.

Prizes and going-away bags

After the party, children expect to go home with a party bag full of goodies. Set a limit to how much you wish to spend and here are some of the things you could buy for party bags. Your child will love helping to make up these bags and from experience I have found it is best that everyone gets the same. However, boys and girls will have different goody bags. You could also wrap up a slice of birthday cake in foil and pop it in the bag too.

Pens, pencils, rubbers, sharpeners, notebooks
Stickers
Hair ornaments
Jewellery
Light stick necklace
Nail varnish
Bead kits
Bubble bath
Packets of seeds
Bubble kits

Marzipan animals
Yoyos
Colouring books
Mini-collage kit
Paper aeroplanes
Badges
Miniature bouncy balls
Silly putty
Mini-magic trick

For prizes, put some of these into a hat and have a lucky dip. If it is a mixed party, have a lucky dip each for girls and boys.

If there are lots of presents for the birthday boy or girl, I know that with my own children I usually allow them to open some after the party and then open one or two a day after that. It is something to look forward to after school. Don't forget to make a list of the presents that everyone has given so that your child can send thank-you notes.

Savoury Party Food

Bashful Sausage Hedgehog

SERVES 8

large black olive, stoned
1 large grapefruit
cocktail sticks
liquorice strips
cocktail sausages

This is quick and easy to assemble and looks great – the sausages will vanish in no time at all.

To make the hedgehog's eyelashes, curl short lengths of liquorice by wrapping them around a pencil and securing with tightly wrapped silver foil. Set aside for 30 minutes for the eyelashes to take shape.

Cut a thin slice off the base of the grapefruit so that it sits flat then, using a sharp knife, make two slits for the eyes and insert the liquorice eyelashes. To form the hedgehog's nose, attach the olive to the grapefruit using half a cocktail stick.

Cook the sausages, spear with cocktail sticks and stick into the grapefruit to form the hedgehog's spikes.

PREVIOUS PAGE
Bashful Sausage Hedgehog

Avocado Frog Dip

You can decorate this tasty and nutritious dip with slices of egg and stuffed olive for the eyes and strips of chives for the mouth. I like to serve it with a selection of raw vegetables and cheese cut into novelty shapes using cookie cutters.

Cut the avocado in half, remove the stone and scoop out the flesh. Mash or blend together all the ingredients and season lightly. Decorate to look like a frog.

SERVES 6

1 large ripe avocado

½ tbsp lemon juice

2 tbsp cream cheese

1 tbsp snipped chives

1 tomato, skinned, de-seeded and chopped

salt and freshly ground black pepper

DECORATION

2 slices cucumber

2 slices hard-boiled egg

2 stuffed olives

2 chives

cheese cut-outs

Crudités with Annabel's Dip

SERVES 8

DIP

50 g (2 oz) finely chopped
onion
100 ml (4 fl oz) vegetable oil
4 tbsp rice wine vinegar
3 tbsp water
1 tbsp chopped fresh ginger
root
2 tbsp chopped celery
2 tbsp soy sauce
3 tsp tomato purée
3 tsp sugar
2 tsp lemon juice
salt and freshly ground black
pepper

This dip is one of my children's favourite things to eat. They love it as a snack when they come home from school and it's been a great way to get them to enjoy eating vegetables. As well as colourful vegetable sticks for a party you could also serve bread sticks or you can use mini-cutters to cut larger vegetables like red peppers or fat carrots into shapes like small stars. The dip also makes a delicious salad dressing.

TO MAKE THE DIP, combine all the ingredients in a blender or food processor and process until smooth. Cut the vegetables into sticks where appropriate and arrange on a plate with the dip served in a bowl on the centre of the plate.

FOR THE CRUDITÉS, chop up any or all of the following vegetables: carrot, cucumber, sweet pepper, celery, gem lettuce, cherry tomatoes, sugar snap peas and cauliflower florets.

Hot Potato Wedges with Sour Cream Dip

Children love eating things that they can pick up with their fingers and dip into a sauce.

Pre-heat the oven to 200°C/400°F/Gas 6. Cut each potato into about six wedges. Place the potatoes in a roasting tin. Toss in the olive oil and sprinkle with the paprika and salt and cook for 35 to 40 minutes, turning a few times.

TO MAKE THE DIP, simply mix together all the ingredients. It's even better to make the dip the day before or at least several hours ahead to leave time for all the flavours to infuse.

MAKES 4 PORTIONS

POTATO WEDGES

450 g (14 oz) medium
    potatoes (Desirée potatoes
    are good for this)
1 tbsp olive oil
½ tsp paprika
½ tsp salt

SOUR CREAM DIP

150 ml (5 fl oz) sour cream or
    crème fraiche
1 tbsp single cream
1 tsp lemon juice
1 tbsp snipped chives
salt and freshly ground black
    pepper

OVERLEAF: Cheese Wands (p40), Sausage Aeroplanes (p36), Magic Toadstools (p36), Hot Potato Wedges with Sour Cream Dip (above)

Sausage Aeroplanes

MAKES 6 AEROPLANES

6 sausages
12 Hula Hoops
12 long thin crispbreads
1 cheese spread in a tube
cheese slices, e.g. Gruyère,
    Cheddar, cut into 12
    triangles

Watch that these sausages don't take off before you manage to grab them!

Grill the sausages. Attach two Hula Hoops to six of the crispbreads using a little of the cheese spread as 'glue' to form the wheels of the plane. Rest the cooked sausages over the crispbreads. Position a second crispbread on top of the sausages and secure with cheese spread to form the other wing. Attach a strip of cheese for the propeller using the cheese spread and form the tails of the planes with triangles of cheese.

Magic Toadstools

MAKES 6 TOADSTOOLS

6 hard-boiled eggs
cheese spread in a tube
3 small tomatoes, halved
salad cress

These are easy to prepare, look fabulous and they are made with healthy ingredients.

Trim the top and bottom of each of the hard-boiled eggs so that they are flat and arrange on a plate. Squeeze or pipe dots of cheese spread over the tomatoes and place a halved tomato on top of each of the boiled eggs. Decorate the plate with salad cress.

Pizza Faces

These make popular party food and it is quite fun to let the children choose the toppings themselves before the pizzas are baked in the oven. It is also fun to decorate the pizzas to look like faces. As a quick alternative, you can use split toasted muffins or bagels for the pizza bases and a ready-made tomato sauce.

Sieve the flour and salt into a bowl and rub in the butter using your fingertips until it resembles fine breadcrumbs. Stir in the cheese and then mix in the milk to form a soft dough. Roll out on a lightly floured work surface to a thickness of about 5 mm (¼ in) and cut out 10 mini pizzas using a 7.5 cm (3 in) cutter.

TO MAKE THE TOMATO SAUCE, melt the butter and sauté the onion for about 4 minutes until soft. Stir in the drained tomatoes, tomato purée, herbs and salt and pepper. Bring to the simmer and cook for about 2 minutes until thickened slightly.

TOP EACH PIZZA with a heaped tablespoon of the tomato sauce. Add a couple of slices of mushrooms, top with some sweetcorn, a slice of tomato and some of the grated mozzarella. Extra toppings could include tuna, ham and olives. Drizzle over a little olive oil. Lay the pizzas on a greased baking tray and bake in an oven preheated to 220°C/425°F/Gas 7 for about 18 minutes.

MAKES 10 PIZZAS

225 g (8 oz) self-raising flour

1 tsp salt

50 g (2 oz) butter

75 g (3 oz) strong Cheddar cheese, grated

6 tbsp milk

TOMATO SAUCE

1 small onion, finely chopped

15 g (½ oz) butter

1 x 400 g (14 oz) can chopped tomatoes, drained

1 tbsp tomato purée

¼ tsp mixed dried herbs

salt and pepper

3 sliced button mushrooms

2 tomatoes, sliced

50 g (2 oz) sweetcorn

90 g (3½ oz) grated mozzarella cheese

1 tbsp olive oil

Cooking Party

COOKING PARTY INVITATIONS
You will need: small wooden spoons, black permanent marker pen, sheets A4 size coloured paper, padded envelopes.

On the handle of the wooden spoon write 'Come to Lara's Cooking Party'. Draw the outline of a rolling pin on coloured paper, cut around the outline and write on the rolling pin the details of the party. Place the rolling pin and wooden spoon inside a padded envelope. Either provide cheap aprons for the children or ask them to bring aprons with them on the invitation.

Children adore cooking and you don't have to wait for a birthday to hold a cooking party. In the school holidays ask your child to invite some friends over and let them choose some favourite recipes to prepare for supper or tea. The children will have the most wonderful time making the dishes, together with a little adult supervision where necessary, and will be very proud to have prepared their own meal, which they might share with their parents if you get lucky.

The perfect age for a cooking party is between 5 and 12 years. However, if you intend it to be a birthday party and want to invite quite a number of children you will really need quite a large kitchen. You may also need to hire or borrow some extra tables for the children to work on to prevent it from becoming a battleground. It will be important to have some adults to assist you in helping the children with their cooking and to do things like putting food in the oven or weighing out ingredients.

There will also be quite a lot of clearing up between recipes. So it is a good idea to have breaks in the cooking when the children can play party games in another room and your helpers can arrange the ingredients so that they are set up ready for the next recipe when the children come back to the kitchen.

Recipes

Plan the recipes with your child. Divide up the ingredients so that children can work in pairs and, where appropriate, weigh out ingredients beforehand and have them ready in small plastic bags or bowls. Have the instructions for each of the recipes printed out on separate pieces of paper in easy steps for the children to follow. Make a little book of recipes with a cover and staple together so that the children can take it home with them afterwards. Before they attempt each recipe, read out the instructions and explain each step carefully to the children.

Once you have chosen the recipes and you know how many children are coming, make a list of all the utensils you will need, such as baking trays, mixing bowls, chopping boards, etc. Borrow some from friends, neighbours, relatives or parents of the children coming to the party and pick them up a couple of days before the party.

Make sure that you take lots of photos as this will be a very memorable party and there are bound to be some great action shots. It's great to see the children sit down and tuck into a tea that they have prepared themselves. You can pack up any extra food in individual boxes so that the children can take it home to their parents who are bound to be very impressed!

IDEAL COOKING PARTY RECIPES
You will probably want to choose four of them.

Pizza Faces (page 37)
Cheese Wands (page 40)
Cheesy Feet and Hands (page 46)
Bagel Snake (page 53)
Chocolate Swiss Roll Aliens (page 60)
Heart-shaped faces (page 64)
Coconut Kisses (page 69)
Apple Smiles (page 70)
Jam tarts (page 86)
Buzzy Bees (page 87)
White Chocolate Rice Krispie Squares (page 88)
Any of the drinks on pages 94-95.

Mini-chicken Burgers

MAKES 15 BURGERS

❄

4 chicken breasts

2 medium onions, peeled and
   grated or finely chopped

3 tbsp tomato ketchup

salt and pepper

50 g (2 oz) fine matzo meal or
   fine breadcrumbs

vegetable oil

These are easy to prepare and are especially good served with oven-baked chips and ketchup.

Cut the chicken into small pieces and put in a food processor with the onion. Chop for a few seconds. Transfer to a mixing bowl and stir in the tomato ketchup, seasoning and 2 tbsp of the fine matzo meal. Using your hands, form the mixture into about 15 burgers and coat with matzo meal. Heat the oil in a large saucepan and fry the burgers for 2 to 3 minutes on each side.

Cheese Wands

MAKES AS MANY AS YOU LIKE

a large grapefruit

aluminium foil

variety of cheeses, eg Cheddar,
   Gruyère, Red Leicester

cucumber, cherry tomatoes

15 cm (6 in) skewers

This is an appealing way to serve some healthy party food.

Cut the base off a large grapefruit so that it is flat, cover with aluminium foil and place in the centre of a serving plate. Cut the cheese into 1 cm (½ in) slices and then cut into star shapes using cookie cutters. Make skewers using chunks of cucumber, cheese stars and cherry tomatoes. Stick the skewers into the grapefruit so that it is evenly covered.

Chicken Nuggets with Potato Crisps

I make these with cheese and onion crisps but you could try other flavours too. These nuggets can be made in advance and then just heated through in the oven.

Cut each chicken breast into about eight pieces and marinate in the lemon juice and garlic for about 30 minutes. Remove the chicken from the marinade, dip each piece first in the seasoned flour, then in the egg and finally in a mixture of the breadcrumbs and crushed crisps. Heat the oil in a large frying pan, add the chicken pieces and sauté for about 5 minutes, turning occasionally until golden and cooked through.

MAKES 16 CHICKEN NUGGETS

2 large chicken breasts
 (approximately 250 g/9 oz)
juice of 1 small lemon
1 small garlic clove, thinly
 sliced
salt and freshly ground black
 pepper
seasoned flour
1 egg, lightly beaten
50 g (2 oz) fresh white
 breadcrumbs
50 g (2 oz) cheese and onion
 crisps, crushed
vegetable oil

Cucumber Crocodile

SERVES 4-6

1 cucumber

mixture of cheeses

1 carrot (optional)

fresh pineapple or 1 small can
   of pineapple chunks

cocktail sticks

2 cherry tomatoes

salad cress (optional)

This looks amazing, it's great for parties and it also makes a fabulous prop for your own children's healthy snacks. I like to use a variety of cheeses, but cubes of ham or chicken also work well in place of the cheese.

Cut out a triangle at one end of the cucumber to make the crocodile's mouth. Cut two lengths of cheese and the carrot (if using) and, with a sharp knife, cut along one side of each length to form a serrated edge. These are the crocodile's teeth. Chop the cheeses and pineapple into cubes. Thread cheese and pineapple cubes on to each cocktail stick and spear the sticks into the cucumber. Cut a cocktail stick in half and use the two halves to attach the cherry tomatoes to form the crocodile's eyes. Give the crocodile some teeth and he's ready to be served up! If you like, you can put him on a bed of salad cress to look like grass.

Mini-beefburgers

These can be served plain or in a bun with some fried onions, lettuce and ketchup. It's also fun to use some ketchup to pipe the first letter of the children's names on top of each bun. It is easy to make a small piping bag out of greaseproof paper for piping the ketchup – the trick is to move your hand quickly to pipe the initial.

Squeeze out some of the liquid from the grated potato, onion and apple so that they are still moist but not too wet. Then mix these together with all the other ingredients and using floured hands, form into mini-burgers. Sauté in vegetable oil and then grill or barbecue until cooked through.

MAKES 15 MINI-BURGERS
❄

1 large potato, peeled and grated

1 onion, peeled and grated

1 large Granny Smith apple, peeled and grated

450 g (1 lb) lean minced beef

1 tbsp chopped fresh parsley

1 crumbled chicken stock cube

40 g (1½ oz) fresh breadcrumbs

½ tsp Marmite

salt and freshly ground black pepper

Sports Party

FOOTBALL PARTY INVITATION
You will need: A4 paper,
pencils and crayons
Design the invitations in the
form of your son's favourite
football team strip. Draw the
football strip on a sheet of A4
paper and write on the strip
the details of the party.
Photocopy as many as you
need, then colour in and cut
out along the outline. The
number on the back could
correspond to your child's age.
It would be fun also to
send a reply card in the
shape and design of
a football.

This is the perfect party for a group of energetic boys. Ideally, it should be an outdoor party, but a hired gym or large hall would be fine too. Plan the party as outlined on pages 12-15.

When choosing the sporting events, ensure you have a mixture of individual and team games. For the latter, it is best to divide the children into more, smaller teams so that the party doesn't become too competitive. Also, spread the talent among the teams so that they are pretty well balanced. Organise a timetable of events and organise all the equipment, such as a long ribbon for the finishing line.

Teams can compete against each other in heats. For example, if there are 24 children, they can be divided into four teams of six. So two teams would compete against each other at a time and then the two winners of the teams would compete to find the overall winner. Award 2 points for the winner and 1 point for the runner-up. Consider holding an Olympic games party and award gold, silver and bronze medals to the amateur athletes.

Adding to the Fun

- For a football match, have a large board with the two teams written on them, calling each a colour. Buy different coloured wide ribbon and tie a length around the arm of each player according to which team they are in.

- Organise some medals, prizes or miniature silver cups for different categories, like best goalie, best striker, best dribbler, boy of the match, which can be handed out after the tea.

Ideas for Sporting Events

4 x 100 metres relay race

Three-legged race

Obstacle course

Jumping balloon race (page 20)

Siamese twins (page 22)

Wheelbarrow race (page 25)

Spud and spoon race (page 25)

Crab race (page 25)

Up and under (page 26)

Dressing-up race (page 26)

IDEAL FOOTBALL PARTY RECIPES

Bashful Sausage Hedgehog (page 30)

Cucumber Crocodile (page 42)

Mini-beefburgers (page 43)

Bagel Snake (page 53)

Tractor Sandwich (page 54)

Football Boot Baguette (page 57)

Chocolate Swiss Roll Aliens (page 60)

My Favourite Chocolate Cake (page 63)

Yummy Jelly Boats (page 73)

Jam Tarts (page 86)

White Chocolate Rice Krispie Squares (page 88)

Cheesy Feet and Hands

MAKES 4

25 g (1 oz) butter
100 g (4 oz) puff pastry sheets
   (frozen uncooked pastry
   sheets, defrosted)
1 egg
100 g (4 oz) grated cheese
tomato purée or tomato
   ketchup

You will need to make templates of feet and hands using a sheet of plastic or card for the children to cut around. Alternatively, you could use biscuit cutters (like animal shapes) to cut out different cheese pastry shapes.

Grease a large baking tray with the butter and set the oven to 200°C/400°F/Gas 6. Sprinkle a clean work surface with a little flour and roll out the pastry with a rolling pin. Prick it with a fork to stop it rising during the cooking. Place the foot and hand templates on the pastry and cut around them. Beat the egg with a fork and brush over the pastry. Sprinkle with the cheese. Lift the feet and hands very carefully on to a greased baking tray. If you like you can decorate the toe- and fingernails with a little tomato purée or ketchup. Bake for 10 to 15 minutes then cool on a wire rack.

Sandwiches

Presentation is very important to a child and fortunately sandwiches can come in many different shapes, sizes and colours. There are many varieties of bread to choose from, such as raisin bread, pitta bread pockets, bagels, bridge rolls. Here are some ideas to make sandwiches look extra special.

NOVELTY-SHAPED SANDWICHES   Use cookie cutters to cut sandwiches into animal shapes, little people, cars, trains, etc. These can be filled sandwiches or open-faced sandwiches.

PINWHEEL SANDWICHES To make a pinwheel sandwich, choose a fairly dense bread and, if you can, chill it first as it will then be easier to handle. Remove the crusts from two slices of bread, then place the slices on a board, with the shorter sides slightly overlapping and roll them together with a rolling pin to join the slices together and to make the bread more pliable. Spread with a contrasting-coloured filling to the colour of the bread – something like smoked salmon and cream cheese mixed with a little tomato ketchup or peanut butter and strawberry jam. Spread with your chosen filling and roll up like a Swiss roll. Using a sharp knife, slice into wheels. If making ahead, wrap tightly with plastic wrap and set aside in the fridge and then slice just before serving.

SPOTTY SANDWICHES To make spotty sandwiches use the end of a piping nozzle to remove small circles from a slice of white and brown bread. Replace the white discs in the holes in the brown bread and the brown discs in the holes in the white bread.

PITTA BREAD POCKETS Warm a small pitta bread in a toaster or pre-heated oven, cut in half and fill with a savoury filling like strips of chicken, turkey with salad or hummus.

peanut butter or strawberry
jam
egg mayonnaise or cucumber
grated Cheddar cheese or ham
Marmite and lettuce or cream
cheese and tomato

DOUBLE-DECKER SANDWICHES Spread a slice of brown bread on both sides with butter and two slices of white bread on one side only. Choose one from a pair of fillings and spread it over one of the slices of white bread. Cover with the brown bread and spread this with the other filling. Put the second slice of white bread on top. Cut off crusts, wrap in plastic wrap and set aside in the fridge until required. Cut into three strips and then each strip into three squares.

Great Sandwich Fillings

Chopped hard-boiled egg mashed with a little soft margarine, mayonnaise and sprinkled with salad cress

Butter, Marmite and shredded lettuce

Cream cheese and cucumber

Peanut butter

Peanut butter, honey and sliced banana

Chocolate spread and banana

Peanut butter and strawberry jam

Grated red Leicester cheese and finely grated carrot mixed with a little mayonnaise

Tuna or salmon mayonnaise with chopped celery or spring onions

Grated Cheddar cheese and mango chutney

Coronation chicken and shredded lettuce

Cream cheese with diced ham

Mashed sardines mixed with a little tomato ketchup

Sliced Swiss cheese, tomato and shredded lettuce

Taramasalata

Small cooked prawns with mayonnaise or Cocktail Sauce (see page 172) and shredded lettuce

Bagel Snake

This is a fun way of arranging sandwiches and I find that bagels are popular with both children and their mums and dads. You can make the snake as long as you like, depending on how many bagels you use, and you can also use a variety of toppings. I have chosen tuna and egg toppings, which are both nutritious but, of course, there are an infinite variety of ingredients that you could choose. For example, consider cream cheese and cucumber or Marmite, grated Cheddar cheese and shredded lettuce.

Slice the bagels in half and then cut each half down the centre to form a semicircle. Cut out the head of the snake from one of the pieces of bagel and the tail from another. Mix the ingredients for the tuna and cheese topping and mix the ingredients for the egg mayonnaise topping. Spread half the bagels with tuna and half with egg.

DECORATE THE TUNA TOPPING with halved cherry tomatoes and the egg topping with strips of chives arranged in a criss-cross pattern. Arrange the bagels to form the body of a snake. Then attach the head to the snake's body and arrange two slices of stuffed olive to form the eyes and cut out a forked tongue from the strip of red pepper.

2 bagels

EGG MAYONNAISE WITH SALAD
  CRESS
2 to 3 hard-boiled eggs (10
  minutes)
3 tbsp mayonnaise
1 tbsp chives
3 tbsp salad cress
salt and freshly ground black
  pepper

DECORATION
cherry tomatoes, halved
chives, 1 stuffed olive, sliced
strip of red pepper

Tractor Sandwich

With a little imagination assorted sandwiches can take on a whole new look.

This makes a great centrepiece for a birthday party and never fails to impress. Simply lay out brown and white bread and spread with different but complementary fillings like those suggested and form into the shape of a tractor. Make the trailer from one and a half bagels, and line up some fresh farm produce like cherry tomatoes, cucumber and celery. Make the wheels from sliced red peppers and carrot slices, the windows from cheese slices and chives (these will stick better if heated for a few seconds in a microwave) and a sesame stick for the funnel. The children will have a great time taking it to pieces.

brown and white sliced bread

fillings, eg egg and cress, ham
   and cheese, cream cheese,
   cucumber and tomato

2 bagels

cherry tomatoes

celery

red peppers, cored, de-seeded
   and sliced

carrots

cheese slices

chives

sesame stick

Funny Fish Sandwich

It takes only a few minutes to transform a simple sandwich into a real show stopper!

Cut the long bread roll open just below the middle and spread both halves with butter or margarine. Lay a few soft lettuce leaves on the bottom half and arrange some slices of boiled egg on top and spread with a little mayonnaise (alternatively use cheese slices). Position two thick slices of tomato so that they protrude a little at one end. Cut a shallow groove along the centre top of the roll and insert three halved cucumber slices to look like fins. Place this on top of the bottom half of the roll and secure two blueberries with toothpicks to make the eyes.

MAKES 1 FISH SANDWICH

1 long soft white roll
butter or margarine
soft lettuce leaves
hard-boiled egg
mayonnaise or cheese slices
1 tomato, sliced
3 slices cucumber
2 blueberries
toothpicks

Football Boot Baguette

These would be great to serve as a snack when a big football game is on and they would be perfect to serve up for a football party. I have chosen a tuna mayonnaise filling, but there are many other choices like cheese and tomato, turkey salad or ham and cheese.

To make the filling, drain and flake the tuna and mix it together with some finely sliced celery and mayonnaise. Cut the baguettes in half lengthways and spread with margarine or butter. Line with lettuce leaves and spoon over some of the filling. Arrange some sliced tomatoes and cucumber on top.

PLACE THE BAGUETTES on halved black olives to represent the studs of the football boots. Thinly slice some of the olives to use as eyelets and place on top of the baguettes. Use thin slices and circles of red pepper to represent laces.

MAKES 4 MINI-BAGUETTES

2 x 200 g (7 oz) cans tuna in oil
1 stick celery, finely chopped
2-3 tbsp mayonnaise
4 small baguettes
margarine or butter
lettuce
tomato slices
cucumber slices
black olives, stoned
1 red pepper

Sweet Party Food

Chocolate Swiss Roll Aliens

MAKE AS MANY AS YOU LIKE

miniature chocolate Swiss rolls

variety of sweets

tubes of coloured writing icing

edible silver balls

Matchmaker chocolate sticks

1 quantity chocolate
  buttercream (see below)

Create your very own edible extraterrestrials.

DECORATE THE SWISS ROLLS as in the photograph on the previous page to look like aliens using a variety of sweets attached with some of the chocolate buttercream.

Chocolate Buttercream

MAKES 1 QUANTITY

25 g (1 oz) softened butter

45 g (1¾ oz) icing sugar

1 tbsp cocoa powder

To make the chocolate buttercream, put the butter into a small bowl. Sift together the icing sugar and cocoa powder and add to the butter. Beat with a wooden spoon until thoroughly mixed.

PREVIOUS PAGE: Chocolate Swiss Roll Aliens

Nicholas's Favourite Marble Cake

My son Nicholas likes to help me make this cake, he really enjoys the bit where you swirl the colours together but I have to temper his enthusiasm or the whole cake can turn a murky brown.

Pre-heat the oven to 170°C/325°F/Gas 3. Cream the butter and sugar together until fluffy. Sieve the almonds and flour and add to the mixture. Gradually beat in the eggs, one at a time, and add the milk. Transfer half the cake mixture to another bowl and stir in the almond essence and orange rind. Melt the chocolate in a microwave or double boiler, and stir the melted chocolate and sifted cocoa powder into the remaining cake mixture.

THIS CAKE LOOKS BEST when baked in a fluted 20 cm (8 in) diameter ring tin. Grease and flour the tin first or use a non-stick baking spray. Alternatively, line a 900 g (2 lb) oblong cake tin or a 20 cm (8 in) diameter tin and pour in the batter. Spoon alternate layers of the cake mixture into the tin and use a skewer or a knife to swirl through the mixture to give a marbled effect. Level the surface and bake for about 1 hour or until the cake is well risen and golden. Turn out on to a wire rack and cool.

SERVES 10

❄ **N**

225 g (8 oz) butter, room temperature

225 g (8 oz) caster sugar

75 g (3 oz) ground almonds

175 g (6 oz) self-raising flour, sifted

4 eggs

3 tbsp milk

1 tsp almond essence

1 tsp finely grated orange rind

75 g (3 oz) plain chocolate, broken into pieces

1 tbsp cocoa powder

Glacé Icing

225 g (8 oz) icing sugar, sifted
1 to 2 tbsp water
a few drops of food colouring
(optional)

These two icings are used on recipes throughout this book. They have excellent 'gluing' properties as well as being useful for decorations.

Sift the icing sugar into a bowl and gradually add the water until the icing is thick enough but is still able to be spread evenly. Add the flavouring or colouring and use immediately.

Royal Icing

1 egg white
approximatelty 225 g (8 oz)
icing sugar, sifted

Beat the egg white with a fork, then gradually beat in half the icing sugar with a wooden spoon until smooth. Add the rest of the icing sugar until you have the desired consistency. Instead of raw egg white, you can use reconstituted dried egg white.

TO MAKE A SMALL PAPER PIPING BAG, cut a 20 cm (8 in) square of greaseproof paper and fold it diagonally to make a triangle. Lift a bottom corner and curl it around to meet the tip of the triangle at the front, then curl the other corner around the back. Fold the point over to secure. Snip off the tip and use as a mini-piping bag.

My Favourite Chocolate Cake

This is the most delicious chocolate cake – moist and lovely and chocolatey. It is also very easy and quick to make.

Pre-heat the oven to 180°C/350°F/Gas 4. Cream together the margarine and sugar until light and fluffy. Beat the eggs and mix with the cocoa powder. Gradually add the egg and cocoa powder to the creamed margarine and sugar. Sift together the flour and baking powder and fold this into the first mixture, then gradually mix in the milk until well blended. Line and grease two 20 cm (8 in) round sandwich tins and spoon the mixture into each of them. Bake for about 30 minutes until risen and slightly firm to the touch. Allow to cool a little, remove from the tins and place on a wire cooling rack.

TO PREPARE THE FUDGE TOPPING, heat the cream in a saucepan until boiling. Remove from the heat and stir in the broken chocolate until melted. Finally, beat in the butter. Allow to cool and place in the fridge for about 30 minutes before using this to sandwich the cakes together and also to cover the top and sides of the cake. Decorate with piped rosettes of double cream, fresh raspberries and mint.

MAKES 8 PORTIONS

❄ without the icing and decoration

100 g (4 oz) soft margarine

300 g (10 oz) soft brown sugar

2 eggs

100 g (4 oz) cocoa powder

200 g (8 oz) self-raising flour

1 tsp baking powder

250 ml (8 fl oz) milk

175 ml (6 fl oz) double cream

200 g (8 oz) plain chocolate

25 g (1 oz) butter, diced

DECORATION

5 fl oz (¼ pint) carton double cream

fresh raspberries

fresh mint leaves

Heart-shaped Faces

MAKES 18 COOKIES

🎅 ❄ without decorations

100 g (4 oz) softened butter

50 g (2 oz) caster sugar

175 g (6 oz) plain flour

pinch of salt

few drops of vanilla essence

ICING

175 g (6 oz) icing sugar, sifted

1½ tbsp lemon juice or water

DECORATION

assorted tubes of writing icing

mini-coloured sugar balls

It's fun to make and decorate these to look like different members of the family and friends for mother's day.

Pre-heat the oven to 180°C/350°F/Gas 4. Beat the butter and sugar together either by hand with a wooden spoon or in an electric mixer at low speed until thoroughly mixed. Sift together the flour and salt and mix this into the butter mixture together with a few drops of vanilla essence to form a fairly stiff dough. If the dough is too dry add a little water.

Form the dough into a ball using your hands and then roll out thinly on a floured work surface using a rolling pin dusted with flour. Cut into heart shapes using biscuit cutters. Collect all the trimmings together and roll these out again to make more biscuits. Arrange on greased or lined baking sheets and bake for about 15 minutes or until the biscuits are lightly golden.

TO MAKE THE ICING, put the icing sugar in a bowl and enough lemon juice or water to make a good spreading consistency. Spread the icing on to the cooled biscuits with a small palette knife. When set decorate each cookie to look like a face.

Carrot and Pineapple Muffins

MAKES 12 REGULAR AND ABOUT 30
MINI-MUFFINS

100 g (4 oz) plain flour

100 g (4 oz) plain wholemeal flour

1 tsp baking powder

¾ tsp bicarbonate of soda

1½ tsp ground cinnamon

½ tsp salt

200 ml (7 fl oz) vegetable oil

90 g (3½ oz) caster sugar

2 eggs

120 g (4½ oz) finely-grated carrots

225 g (8 oz) can crushed pineapple, semi-drained

100 g (4 oz) raisins

These are probably my favourite muffins; they are wonderfully moist with an irresistible taste. They make a good snack any time of the day and also make great mini-muffins for parties. It is a good idea to cut the raisins in half when making mini-muffins.

Pre-heat the oven to 180°C/350°F/Gas 4. Sift together the flours, baking powder, bicarbonate of soda, cinnamon and salt and mix well. Beat the oil, sugar and eggs until well blended. Add the grated carrots, crushed pineapple and raisins. Gradually add the flour mixture, beating just enough to combine all the ingredients.

POUR THE BATTER INTO MUFFIN TRAYS lined with paper cases and bake for 25 minutes for regular muffins and 15 to 17 minutes for mini-muffins. Cool on a wire rack. A fan-assisted oven will cook food faster than a conventional oven. If you cook in such an oven, you will need to reduce the oven temperature by 10-20°C/20-50°F/Gas 1.

Baked Alaska

This looks sensational but it really is not difficult to make.

Leave the ice creams out of the freezer until slightly softened. Take a 600 ml (1 pint) pudding mould or use a plastic dome shaped container and line with plastic wrap (this will make it easier to remove the ice cream once it has hardened). Fill two-thirds with strawberry ice cream, smooth over the surface and then fill the remainder of the container with vanilla ice cream. Set aside in the freezer until the ice cream is really hard.

Pre-heat the oven to 200°C/400°F/Gas 6. Slice the Swiss roll into 1 cm (¼ in) thick slices. Lightly grease a baking tray and arrange a circle of Swiss roll slices to fit the base of the Baked Alaska. Remove the ice cream from the mould and cover with the rest of the Swiss roll slices. Place the ice cream on top of the base and put in the freezer. Separate the eggs and beat the whites until they form stiff peaks. Add half the caster sugar, a tablespoon at a time, whisking after each addition. Fold in the remaining sugar using a metal spoon.

FOR THE DRAMATIC END RESULT, remove the ice-cream mould from the freezer, cover with the egg whites and fluff up with a fork. Bake in the oven for about 5 minutes until the surface of the meringue has hardened and the peaks are lightly golden.

MAKES 6 PORTIONS

❆ after cookng the meringue

1 x 600 ml (1 pint) carton strawberry ice cream (not soft scoop)

1 x 600 ml (1 pint) carton vanilla ice cream (not soft scoop)

1 raspberry Swiss roll

3 eggs

150 g (5 oz) caster sugar

Annabel's Apricot Cookies

MAKES 26 COOKIES

❄

100 g (4 oz) unsalted butter

100 g (4 oz) cream cheese

100 g (4 oz) caster sugar

75 g (3 oz) plain flour

50 g (2 oz) chopped dried
apricots

65 g (2½ oz) white chocolate
chips or chopped white
chocolate

This fabulous and rather unusual combination of dried apricots and white chocolate makes irresistible cookies. Once you have sampled these you will probably want to double the quantities second time around.

Pre-heat the oven to 180°C/350°F/Gas 4. In a large mixing bowl, cream together the butter and cream cheese. Add the sugar and beat until fluffy. Gradually add the flour, then fold in the apricots and chocolate. The dough will be quite soft – don't worry!

DROP HEAPED TEASPOONS OF THE MIXTURE on to baking sheets and bake for 15 minutes or until lightly golden. Allow the cookies to cool and harden for a few minutes before removing from the baking sheet.

Coconut Kisses

I defy you to eat only one of these! They are definitely one of my favourites, and your children will enjoy helping you make them as well as eat them.

Pre-heat the oven to 180°C/350°F/Gas 4. Cream together the butter and sugars. Add the egg and vanilla. Sift together the flour, baking soda and salt and beat this into the mixture. Stir in the chocolate chips, oats and coconut.

FORM INTO WALNUT SIZED BALLS, flatten the top with your hand and place spaced apart on a lightly greased or lined baking tray. Bake for 10 to 15 minutes. The biscuits will harden when they cool down.

MAKES 25 BISCUITS

N ❄

100 g (4 oz) butter

50 g (2 oz) soft brown sugar

50 g (2 oz) caster sugar

1 egg, beaten

½ tsp pure vanilla extract

75 g (3 oz) plain flour

½ tsp baking soda

½ tsp salt

120 g (4½ oz) plain chocolate chips

75 g (3 oz) rolled oats

40 g (1½ oz) desiccated coconut

Apple Smiles

MAKES 4 APPLE SMILES
N

1 red apple, cored and sliced
   into eighths
a squeeze of lemon juice
smooth peanut butter
miniature marshmallows or
   small cubes of cheese (for a
   healthier alternative)
dried apricots (optional)

This snack is easy to prepare and will certainly bring a smile to your child's face! For a healthier variation, use small cubes of banana instead of mini-marshmallows.

Spread peanut butter on one side of each apple slice (squeeze a little lemon juice over the apple if not serving immediately). Place five miniature marshmallows or cubes of cheese on one apple slice and then lay another apple slice, peanut butter side down, on top. If you like, add an apricot to form the tongue.

Divinely Decadent Fruity Dark Chocolate Bars

These no-bake chocolate fruit and nut bars are amazingly good and one of my favourite treats. They are also fun for children to make.

Break the chocolate into squares and cut the butter into pieces and put these into a large heatproof bowl and place over a saucepan of simmering water, stirring occasionally until melted. Stir the condensed milk into the chocolate mixture and mix in the broken biscuits, chopped peaches or apricots, raisins and chopped pecans.

TO MAKE THE BARS, line an 18 x 28 cm (7 x 11 in) shallow cake tin with plastic wrap, allowing the sides to overhang. Spoon the mixture into the tin and press down but still leave the top a little rough. Set aside in the fridge to set. Once set, lift the cake out of the tin by the overhanging plastic wrap and cut into bars. Keep chilled in the fridge.

MAKES 12 BARS

N

300 g (10 oz) good quality plain chocolate

100 g (4 oz) unsalted butter

1 x 397 g (14 oz) can condensed milk

225 g (8 oz) digestive biscuits, broken into pieces

100 g (4 oz) no-soak dried peaches (or apricots), chopped

50 g (2 oz) raisins

75 g (3 oz) pecans, roughly chopped

Glossy Dark and White Chocolate Brownies

MAKES 16 SQUARES

150 g (5 oz) dark chocolate, chopped

75 g (3 oz) unsalted butter

1 tsp pure vanilla extract

100 g (4 oz) caster sugar

2 eggs

1 egg yolk

90 g (3½ oz) plain flour

¼ tsp salt

150 g (5 oz) white chocolate buttons

CHOCOLATE SATIN GLAZE

75 g (3 oz) dark chocolate, chopped

15 g (½ oz) unsalted butter

50 g (2 oz) white chocolate buttons

Two chocolates are combined to make these irresistible squares of rich, chewy brownies.

Pre-heat the oven to 180°C/350°F/Gas 4 and line and grease a 20 cm (8 in) square baking pan. Melt the dark chocolate and butter in a microwave for 2 minutes on High (or in a saucepan over a gentle heat, stirring constantly). Stir in the vanilla and sugar, then add the eggs and yolk, one at a time, stirring after each addition. Sift together the flour and salt and mix this into the chocolate mixture with the white chocolate buttons. Pour the batter into the prepared pan and bake in the oven for about 30 minutes.

TO PREPARE THE GLAZE, melt the dark chocolate and butter together in a small heatproof bowl over a pan of simmering water and spread over the cake. Melt the white chocolate in a bowl over a pan of simmering water and with a teaspoon trail five lines horizontally across the cake about 1 cm (½ in) apart. Alternatively, pipe lines of white chocolate. Then, with a blunt knife draw vertical lines through the chocolate topping to create a pattern.

Yummy Jelly Boats

These jelly boats are probably the most popular party food that I make.

Squeeze the juice from the oranges and reserve for fresh juice to drink. Carefully scrape out the membrane and discard, taking care not to make a hole in the skin of the orange. Make up the jelly according to the packet instructions and fill each of the hollow orange halves with jelly right to the top. Refrigerate until set and then cut the oranges in half again with a sharp wet knife. Cut triangles out of the rice paper and secure with cocktail sticks to make sails.

MAKES 8 JELLY BOATS

2 large oranges, halved

1 x 135 g (4½ oz) packet fruit jelly, eg strawberry or orange

2 sheets rice paper

8 cocktail sticks

Almond Crescents

MAKES 60 ALMOND CRESCENTS

🍪 **N**

225 g (8 oz) vegetable
    shortening

40 g (1½ oz) icing sugar

1 tbsp water

250 g (9 oz) plain flour

¼ tsp salt

2 tsp vanilla extract

125 g (4½ oz) blanched
    almonds, ground in a food
    processor (but not too fine)

sifted icing sugar

These biscuits are so light they melt in the mouth and are truly delicious. If you don't want to make all the biscuits just use half the dough, wrap the remainder in plastic wrap and keep it in the fridge. It will still be good for three or four days for making a fresh batch of biscuits.

Pre-heat the oven to 150°C/300°F/Gas 2. Cut the shortening into cubes and mix together with the icing sugar and water (this can be done in a food processor). Stir in the flour, salt, vanilla and freshly ground almonds and mix well.

USING YOUR HANDS, roll the dough into pencil-thin lengths of about 7.5 cm (3 in) and form them into crescent shapes with rounded ends. Bake on ungreased baking sheets for 20 minutes. While still warm, roll the biscuits in icing sugar. They are quite delicate so will need careful handling.

Macaroons

As a child I loved macaroons, particularly the rice paper at the bottom. These will taste even more delicious if you grind the almonds yourself by chopping blanched almonds very finely in a food processor.

Pre-heat the oven to 180°C/350°F/Gas 4. Separate the eggs (you will not need the yolks for this recipe) and whisk the egg whites until they form stiff peaks. Gently fold in the almonds, sugar and a few drops of the almond essence. Line two large baking trays with the rice paper.

ROLL THE MIXTURE INTO SMALL BALLS using floured hands and arrange on the rice paper leaving enough room for them to spread during cooking. The mixture will be very sticky so you can chill it in the fridge for 30 minutes before handling so that it has a chance to firm up. Leave to cool on the rice paper, then cut around the macaroons to trim off the excess paper.

MAKES ABOUT 22 MACAROONS

N

2 medium eggs

175 g (6 oz) ground almonds

175 g (6 oz) caster sugar

few drops almond essence

4 sheets rice paper

Pink Meringue Shells

These look like oyster shells with pearls inside them. Present them on a plate with a Little Mermaid doll in the centre.

Pre-heat the oven to 110°C/225°F/Gas ¼. Whisk the egg whites until firm. Carry on whisking, adding 1 tablespoon of the sugar at a time and using up half the sugar. Using a wooden spoon, fold in the remaining sugar together with a few drops of the pink food colouring. Spoon the mixture into a piping bag fitted with a 15 mm (½ in) star nozzle. Pipe about 40 small shell shapes on to baking trays lined with non-stick baking paper. Bake the meringues in an oven for about 1 hour 40 minutes or until crisp. Arrange the meringues on a wire rack to cool.

TO CREATE THE FINISHED EFFECT, whip the cream until it forms stiff peaks and use it to sandwich together pairs of meringue shells. Use edible silver balls to look like pearls in the middle of the open shells.

MAKES 20 PAIRS OF MERINGUE SHELLS

3 egg whites
175 g (6 oz) caster sugar
few drops pink food colouring
250 ml (8 fl oz) double cream
edible silver balls

Tip

Egg whites will whisk better for meringue if they are at room temperature. So take them out of the fridge an hour or so before use.

Make-up and Jewellery Party

MAKE-UP PARTY INVITATIONS
You will need: stiff bright coloured card, metallic silver foil or kitchen foil, glue, stick-on-gems or mini foil stickers. Draw an 18 cm (7 in) circle with a handle on the coloured card and cut out. To make the mirror, draw a 15 cm (6 in) circle on silver metallic wrapping paper or silver foil and cut out. Stick on to the centre of the mirror frame. Decorate the handle with stick-on-gems or mini foil stickers. Write the details on the back of the mirror along the lines of: 'You are invited to Scarlett's Make-up and Jewellery Party at Scarlett's Beauty Salon (address, date and time). To make your appointment call (tel no).'

This party will indulge every little girl's fantasy – after all, if your daughters are anything like my two girls, they can't wait to see what they would look like wearing make-up, high heels and mummy's costume jewellery.

Decide on how many children you want to invite and you will probably want to make this an all girls' party. You can ask them to wear their most trendy outfit on the invitation.

Start collecting inexpensive make-up like glittery nail varnish, nail polish remover, eye shadow, mascara, lipstick, make-up brushes, hair ornaments, spray-on hair colour, etc. Also ask your friends if they have any make-up they don't want any more. Have some towels to drape around the children's shoulders to protect their clothes as they are made up.

You will need some helpers – teenage girls would be great to assist you in the beauty salon. Try to organise it so that the children have a big mirror in front of them so that they can see what is going on.

Organise different areas for make-up, hair and nail polish. While the girls are waiting their turn, have a collection of beads and thread for them to make necklaces and bracelets to wear.

Once everyone has been made up, serve the tea and after tea you could organise party games. It is a good idea to take 'before' and 'after' photographs of each of the children. You could make a little booth in a corner of a room with a chair and a sign behind it saying Scarlett's Beauty Salon. When the photographs are developed, send them out with your daughter's thank-you cards.

Adding to the Fun

Have an appointment book where the children book who they want to do their make-up, hair and nails and give them a number so that they know when it is their turn.

Tilted Jellies

This looks fantastic and everyone will want to know how you got the jelly to set in diagonal stripes. If you like, you can add some fruit like tinned mandarins or raspberries to the various jellies but when it comes to green, don't use kiwi as it contains something that prevents jelly from setting.

MAKES 4 TALL GLASSES

4 x half 135 g (4½ oz) packets
   assorted jellies, eg
   strawberry, lime,
   blackcurrant and orange
4 scoops ice cream
hundreds and thousands

Make up the half packets of jellies in separate bowls according to the packet instructions. Divide the strawberry jelly among four tall glasses and then chill the glasses in the fridge set at an angle. Repeat with the next two jellies, each time propping the glasses at an angle so that the jelly sets on a diagonal and allow setting time between each. Pour in the last jelly and this time stand the glass upright. When the last jelly has set, add a scoop of ice cream and decorate with hundreds and thousands.

Goldfish Bowl Jelly

If you really want to make this look like the real thing, you could always put a few drops of edible blue food colouring into the jelly.

Make up the jelly according to the instructions on the packet. Pour one of the jellies into a round glass bowl that looks like a goldfish bowl. Set aside in the fridge until almost set and then push about six of the fish-shaped sweets into the jelly so that they look as though they are swimming around in the bowl. Place in the fridge until almost set. Pour over the remaining jelly and then return to the fridge until completely set.

MAKES 1 GOLDFISH BOWL

2 x 135 g (4½ oz) packets
  yellow or green jelly
colourful fish-shaped sweets

OVERLEAF: Chocolate Profiterole Cats (p84), Goldfish Bowl Jelly (see above)

Chocolate Profiterole Cats

MAKES 11 LARGE AND 11 SMALL
  PROFITEROLES OR 11 CAT
  PROFITEROLES

❄ without the chocolate

75 g (3 oz) butter

225 ml (8 fl oz) water

100 g (4 oz) plain flour, sifted

50 g (2 oz) caster sugar

pinch salt

3 eggs, lightly beaten

125-150 g (4½-5 oz) plain or
  milk chocolate

1 x 500 ml (1 pint) tub good-
  quality ice cream

DECORATION

tube black writing icing

mini Smarties

whole almonds

black liquorice laces

It's not difficult to make choux pastry for profiteroles. By fitting a plain round nozzle into a piping bag you can also pipe the pastry into mini-éclairs and fill with ice cream. For a real novelty, make large and small rounds of pastry and stack these on top of each other to look like a pussy cat. These cats can be made ahead and frozen and then all you will need to do is add the finishing touches to the decoration.

To make the choux pastry, pre-heat the oven to 200°C/400°F/ Gas 6. Put the butter and water in a saucepan and slowly bring to the boil. Sift the flour on to a sheet of greaseproof or baking paper – this will enable you to slide it in all at once, which is important for making a smooth mixture. Add the flour, caster sugar and salt and then beat vigorously with a wooden spoon until the mixture comes away from the sides of the saucepan. Allow to cool slightly and beat in half the eggs. Gradually beat in the remainder of the eggs (you may not need to use all of the eggs) to make a glossy smooth dough that has a thick dropping consistency.

Drop 11 dessertspoonfuls and 11 smaller spoonfuls of the mixture on to two large greased and floured baking sheets. (They will increase in size quite a bit once they are cooked.)

Bake for 25 minutes until risen and golden. Pierce each bun with a skewer or the point of a sharp knife to release the steam, then return to the oven for 5 to 10 minutes to crisp up. Cool the buns on a wire rack.

When cool, cut a slit in the profiteroles and fill with some of the vanilla ice cream. Pop them in the freezer while you melt the chocolate over a pan of simmering water. Dip each of the profiteroles in the melted chocolate to coat the top of the buns.

TO MAKE CAT PROFITEROLES, attach a small bun on top of a larger bun with a little of the melted chocolate. With the black writing icing, draw a line down the centre of green Smarties and stick these on the face for eyes and use pink Smarties for the nose. Make two little slits in the top of the small bun and stick in almonds for the ears. Finish off by attaching a strip of liquorice for each cat's tail. Store in the freezer and allow to defrost a little before eating.

Jam Tarts

MAKES 24 JAM TARTS

225 g (8 oz) plain flour
pinch of salt
150 g (5 oz) butter, diced
75 g (3 oz) icing sugar
1 egg, lightly beaten
strawberry, raspberry, cherry or
  other jam of your choice

These have always been a real favourite with children and nothing tastes quite as good as the homemade version.

Sift the flour and salt together. Rub in the butter until the mixture resembles fine breadcrumbs. Mix in the icing sugar. Stir in the egg until the mixture forms a soft dough. Mould into a ball using your hands and wrap in plastic wrap. Set aside in the fridge for about 30 minutes; this prevents the pastry from shrinking when it is baked.

TO MAKE THE TARTS, roll out the dough on a lightly floured surface and cut into about 24 circles using a 9 cm (3½ in) round fluted cutter. Press the circles of dough into two lightly greased bun trays and put back in the fridge for about 20 minutes. Pre-heat the oven to 200°C/400°F/Gas 6. Fill each case with about 2 teaspoons of jam and bake for about 15 minutes.

Buzzy Bees

These tasty bees are great fun for parties and they are just the right size for little children. They are packed full of nutritious ingredients and older children will also enjoy making them because they are quick and easy to make and need no cooking. You may want to double the quantity next time around since these bees will keep your children buzzing around for more.

Mix together the peanut butter and honey and then blend in the remaining ingredients. Form heaped teaspoons of the mixture into oval shapes to look like bees. Dip a toothpick into the cocoa powder and press gently on to the bees' bodies to form stripes.

Press rice paper wings or flaked almonds into the sides of the bee. Cut the currants in half, roll between your finger and thumb to form tiny balls and arrange on the bees to look like eyes. The bees can be stored in the fridge for several days.

MAKES 10 BEES

N

4 tbsp smooth peanut butter

1 tbsp honey

2 tbsp dried skimmed milk powder

1 tbsp sesame seeds

1 Weetabix, crushed

DECORATION

1 tbsp cocoa powder

rice paper cut into the shape of wings or flaked almonds

10 currants

White Chocolate Rice Krispie Squares

MAKES 12 SQUARES

75 g (3 oz) butter

100 g (4 oz) golden syrup

60 g (2½ oz) white chocolate chips

100 g (4 oz) Rice Krispies

25 g (1 oz) pastel coloured miniature marshmallows

For those with less than ten minutes to spare, here is a great recipe that is adored by my three children.

Put the butter, golden syrup and white chocolate into a small saucepan and melt together over a low heat. Transfer to a bowl or jug and set aside to cool. Mix together the Rice Krispies and marshmallows and stir in the golden syrup mixture. Line a fairly shallow 20 cm (8 in) square baking tin, spoon in the mixture and level the surface. Cut into squares and store in the fridge.

Rice Krispie Squares

MAKES 16 SQUARES

3 x 65 g (2½ oz) Mars Bars

75 g (3 oz) butter

75 g (3 oz) Rice Krispies

50 g (2 oz) raisins

Here is a fine and tasty variation on the theme.

Cut the Mars Bars into pieces, put into a saucepan with the butter and melt over a low heat. In a bowl, combine the Rice Krispies and raisins. Stir the melted Mars Bar into the Rice Krispies until well coated. Press into a tin, and finish as above.

Chocolate and Toffee Rice Krispie Squares

Here is a truly scrumptious recipe for your children to share among their friends.

Line the base of a shallow 20 cm (8 in) square tin and grease the sides. Put the syrup, sugar and butter in a saucepan and stir over a gentle heat until melted. Remove from the heat and stir in the Rice Krispies. Press this mixture into the prepared tin.

TO MAKE THE FILLING, put the toffees, butter and cream into a saucepan. Stir over a gentle heat until melted. Bring to the boil and pour this over the Rice Krispie mixture. Put in the fridge to set for about 1 hour.

FOR THE TOPPING, break the chocolate into pieces and put it into a heatproof bowl together with the butter. Place over a pan of simmering water and stir until melted. Alternatively, melt the chocolate and butter in a suitable dish in the microwave. Spread the topping over the toffee filling and set aside in the fridge for about 1 hour until set. Carefully remove from the tin and peel off the paper and cut into squares. Store in the fridge.

MAKES 16 SQUARES

125 g (4 oz) golden syrup
50 g (2 oz) soft light brown
    sugar
40 g (1½ oz) butter
50 g (2 oz) Rice Krispies

TOFFEE FILLING
175 g (6 oz) cream toffees
50 g (2 oz) butter
3 tbsp double cream

TOPPING
75 g (3 oz) milk or plain
    chocolate
25 g (1 oz) butter

This Little Piggy Went to the Party

SERVES 10

1 round watermelon
1 cantaloupe melon
1 ogen or honeydew melon
round black and white grapes
assorted fruits

DECORATION
2 large limes
2 glacé cherries
2 raisins

This is such an amazing way to serve fruit and is always greeted with squeals of delight!

First mark out with a pencil or pen the spiral tail of the pig on the watermelon. Cut around the spiral tail and then cut out a large round hole from the top of the melon. Remove the cut-out sections and from this cut a 5 cm (2 in) diameter circle for the snout of the pig and two triangles for the ears. Stick two melon seeds into the centre of the snout for the nostrils and set aside.

Using a melon ball scoop, scoop out watermelon balls until the shell is empty. Discard the seeds as you go. Scrape out any remaining melon and drain the shell of juice. Mop up any remaining juices inside the shell with absorbent kitchen paper. Cut the other two melons in half, remove the seeds and scoop out balls of melo. Add to the watermelon balls in a large bowl.

TO DECORATE THE WATERMELON, halve the limes and attach with toothpicks for the trotters. Attach the snout and ears with toothpicks. Slice the end off the cherries, push a raisin into the centre of each and attach with toothpicks to form the eyes. Drain any liquid from the fruits and fill the watermelon shell.

White Chocolate-chunk Cookies

MAKES 20 COOKIES

🍳 **N** ❄

100 g (4 oz) unsalted butter

100 g (4 oz) caster sugar

100 g (4 oz) soft brown sugar

1 egg

1 tsp vanilla essence

175 g (6 oz) plain flour

½ tsp baking powder

¼ tsp salt

175 g (6 oz) white chocolate,
   broken into small chunks

75 g (3 oz) pecans or walnuts,
   finely chopped (optional)

These are very easy to make and one of my favourite biscuits. They should be quite soft when they are taken out of the oven so that when they cool down they are crisp on the outside but moist and chewy inside. Leave out the nuts for young children.

Pre-heat the oven to 190°C/375°F/Gas 5. Beat the butter together with the sugars. With a fork, beat the egg together with the vanilla essence and add this to the butter mixture. In a bowl, mix together the flour, baking powder and salt. Add this to the butter and egg mixture and blend well. Mix in the chunks of white chocolate and the nuts (if using).

TO MAKE THE COOKIES, line several baking sheets with non-stick baking paper. Using your hands, form the dough into walnut-sized balls and arrange on the baking sheets spaced well apart. Bake in the oven for 10 to 12 minutes. Allow to cool for a few minutes and then transfer to a wire rack.

Blondies

These are called blondies and not brownies because they are made with white chocolate. Brownies always crack a little on the surface so, if you like, you can sift some icing sugar over the surface. To cut the brownies into neat squares, put the whole cake on a board when it has cooled completely and cut into nine large or sixteen smaller squares. The blondies will keep for up to a week in an airtight container.

Pre-heat the oven to 190°C/375°F/Gas 5 and grease and line a 20 cm (8 in) square baking tin. Melt 100 g (4 oz) of the white chocolate with the butter in a heatproof bowl over a pan of simmering water. Set aside to cool down. Beat the eggs with the sugar until smooth, then gradually beat in the melted chocolate mixture. Sift together the flour and salt, then fold into the egg mixture together with the remaining white chocolate, pecans and vanilla essence.

MAKE THE BLONDIES by spooning the mixture into the prepared tin and level the surface with a spatula. Bake in the oven for 30 to 35 minutes until risen and golden and the centre is just firm to the touch. Leave to cool in the tin then turn out on to a wire rack. When completely cool cut into squares.

MAKES 9 LARGE OR 16 SMALL BROWNIES

N

300 g (10 oz) white chocolate, chopped

75 g (3 oz) butter, cut into cubes

3 eggs

175 g (6 oz) caster sugar

175 g (6 oz) self-raising flour

pinch of salt

100 g (4 oz) chopped pecans

1 tsp vanilla essence

Party Drinks

Serve any of these drinks with orange or pineapple slices and maraschino cherries on cocktail sticks, paper umbrellas and fancy straws. These drinks are also fun for children to mix up themselves.

Exotic Fruit Cocktail

MAKES 2 GLASSES

175 ml (6 fl oz) lemonade

125 ml (4 fl oz) mixed tropical fruit juice

2 tbsp grenadine syrup

2 wedges of pineapple

2 maraschino cherries

This looks good because the colours of the drink separate due to the different densities of the liquid. You could also make pink lemonade by mixing lemonade with a little of the grenadine syrup.

Pour the lemonade into two glasses, pour the fruit juice down the side, then pour a tablespoon of the grenadine syrup down the side of each glass. Decorate with a wedge of pineapple and a cherry on a cocktail stick and add a straw.

Strawberry Milkshake

MAKES 2 GLASSES

4 scoops strawberry ice cream

250 ml (8 fl oz) milk

paper umbrellas

straws

Soften two scoops of ice cream, slowly add the milk and stir well. Pour into two glasses and add a scoop of ice cream to each. Place an umbrella in the ice cream and add a straw.

Ice-cream Soda

Blend together the fruit cocktail, lemonade and two scoops of the vanilla ice cream. Pour into two tall glasses, place a scoop of ice cream on top of each and add a straw and the orange and cherry on a cocktail stick for decoration.

MAKES 2 GLASSES

150 g (5 oz) can fruit cocktail (drained)
300 ml (½ pint) lemonade
4 scoops vanilla ice cream
2 slices orange
2 maraschino cherries

Chocolate Malted Milkshake

Cut the Mars Bars into pieces and put them in a suitable dish together with 2 tablespoons of the milk and microwave on High for 2 minutes, then stir. Put the rest of the milk into a saucepan together with the Ovaltine and heat, stirring, but do not boil until dissolved. Add the melted Mars Bars and stir to combine. Remove from the heat and set aside to cool and then put in the fridge. Serve over crushed ice.

MAKES 3 GLASSES

2 x 65 g (2½ oz) Mars Bars
400 ml (⅔ pint) milk
4 tbsp Ovaltine powder
6 crushed ice cubes

Cookies 'n' Cream Shake

Combine the milk, cookies and ice cream in a blender or liquidiser and whizz until smooth. Pour into 6 glasses.

MAKES 6 GLASSES

600 ml (1 pint) milk
6 Oreo cookies, crushed
4 scoops vanilla ice cream

Birthday Cakes

The Three Bears' Cake

SPONGE CAKE

❄ sponge. before decorating

225 g (8 oz) margarine

225 g (8 oz) caster sugar

4 eggs

1 tsp vanilla extract

½ tsp grated lemon rind

225 g (8 oz) self-raising flour

BUTTERCREAM

100 g (4 oz) softened butter

15 ml (1 tbsp) milk

2.5 ml (½ tsp) vanilla essence

225 g (8 oz) icing sugar, sifted

This is a wonderful cake to make for a young child's birthday. Continue the teddy bear theme of Goldilocks and the Three Bears using some of the recipes from the Teddy Bear's Picnic on pages 134-143.

Pre-heat the oven to 170°C/325°F/Gas 3. Lightly grease the base and sides of a 30 x 23 x 2.5 cm (12 x 9 x 1 in) cake tin and line with baking paper. To make the sponge, cream together the margarine and caster sugar until light and fluffy. Gradually beat in the eggs one at a time adding 1 tablespoon of flour with each egg to stop the mixture curdling. Beat in the vanilla extract and the grated lemon rind. Spoon into the prepared tin, level the surface with a palette knife and cook for 30 minutes or until a skewer inserted in the centre comes out clean. Cool slightly, then turn on to a cooling rack, peel off the paper and leave to cool.

Take a 25 x 36 cm (10 x 14 in) cake board and brush lightly with jam. Roll out the pale blue icing thinly and use it to cover the board, trimming the edges and then making a fringe with a sharp knife. Leave to harden.

TO MAKE THE BUTTERCREAM, cream the butter together with the milk and vanilla essence and gradually work in the sifted icing sugar. Beat the icing until light and fluffy.

PREVIOUS PAGE
The Three Bears' Cake

CUT THE SPONGE INTO THREE BEDS of decreasing size (approximately 18 x 10 cm, 14 x 7.5 cm, 10 x 6 cm/7 x 4 in, 5½ x 3 in, 4 x 2½ in). Cut these in half and sandwich together with buttercream and jam. Arrange the cakes on the board and brush the beds with warmed apricot jam. Roll out icing to cover the top third of each bed. Cut out three small rectangles of sponge from the remains of the sponge cake and cover each pillow with ready to roll icing.

Make body shapes for each of the teddy bears using 225 g (8 oz) of the yellow marzipan and place on the beds. Roll out bedspreads and drape them over each bed and trim. Add strips of icing for the turned-down sheets. Shape three bears' heads and paws in decreasing size from yellow marzipan and decorate their faces with black writing icing. Place them on each pillow.

CUT OUT THREE CURVED HEADBOARDS of decreasing size from a circular cake board. Brush the headboards with a little warmed apricot jam. Gather the icing trimmings and divide into two. Colour one batch a darker blue with a few drops of food colouring and roll out to cover the daddy bear's headboard. Also make him a pair of matching blue slippers. Colour the second batch of trimmings pink and roll out to cover the mummy bear's headboard and decorate the top with sugar flowers. Also make a pair of slippers and decorate with sugar flowers, sticking them in place with a little jam. Roll out the remaining yellow marzipan to cover the baby bear's headboard and make him a pair of matching slippers and decorate with a liquorice sweet.

DECORATION
strawberry or raspberry jam
500 g (1 lb) pale blue ready-
    to-roll icing (or colour white
    icing blue using a little food
    colouring)
1 kg (2 lb 4 oz) white ready-
    to-roll icing
pink and blue edible food
    colouring
45 ml (3 tbsp) apricot jam
325 g (10½ oz) yellow
    marzipan

Fairy Princess Cake

N ❄ sponge cake only

175 g (6 oz) butter, softened

150 g (5 oz) soft margarine

275 g (10 oz) caster sugar (or
use 275 g/10 oz) vanilla
sugar and leave out the
vanilla essence)

6 eggs

225 g (8 oz) self-raising flour

½ tsp baking powder

pinch of salt

100 g (4 oz) ground almonds

5 ml (1 tsp) vanilla essence

5 ml (1 tsp) almond essence

BUTTERCREAM

175 g (6 oz) unsalted butter,
softened

250 g (9 oz) icing sugar, sifted

grated rind of 2 lemons

Decoration ingredients are
given overleaf

This is not a difficult cake to make but it looks quite spectacular. My friend Nicky Mallows, who is an artist, made up this cake for her daughter Laura's fourth birthday. My daughter Scarlett was so taken with the cake that she wanted exactly the same for her birthday, and no other cake would do! So Nicky showed me how she made it and now I will share that recipe with you to make every little girl's dream come true. If you wish, you can make the cake ahead of the party and pop it in the freezer before decorating.

Pre-heat the oven to 180°C/350°F/Gas 4. Beat the butter, margarine and sugar together until light and fluffy. Beat in the eggs one at a time together with 1 tablespoon of flour to stop the mixture curdling. Mix in the remaining flour, baking powder and salt. Fold in the ground almonds, vanilla and almond essences until thoroughly blended. Pour the mixture into a greased and floured 1.2 litre (2 pint), 17 cm (6½ in) diameter pudding basin and a 20 cm (8 in) ring mould. Bake for 20 minutes, then reduce the heat to 170°C/325°F/Gas 3 and bake for a further 25 minutes for the ring mould and about 40 minutes for the pudding basin (test with a skewer to make sure the cake is cooked). The ring mould will take less time to cook

6 tbsp apricot jam

500 g (10 oz) golden
marzipan

1 kg (2 lb 4 oz) white ready-
to-roll icing

1 egg white

200 g (7 oz) icing sugar plus
extra for rolling

a little lemon juice

iced flowers

pink food colouring

multi-coloured iced gem
biscuits

edible gold balls

1 feather

1 small doll

1 pink Part Ring iced biscuit

1 paper umbrella

than the pudding basin and will need to be removed from the oven first. Allow the cakes to cool on a wire rack.

MEANWHILE PREPARE THE BUTTERCREAM. Cream the butter and sifted icing sugar in an electric mixer (or use a bowl and wooden spoon), then beat in the grated lemon rind. Cut the pudding basin cake horizontally into three sections and the one from the ring mould horizontally in half. Sandwich these layers together with the buttercream icing. Gently warm the apricot jam, either in a saucepan or in the microwave. Brush the ring mould cake with a little warm apricot jam and place the pudding basin sponge on top. Brush the entire surface of the cake with half the apricot jam.

ON A PLASTIC-WRAP COVERED WORK SURFACE lightly dusted with icing sugar, roll out the marzipan to form a large circle big enough to cover the cake. Lift the marzipan with the aid of the plastic wrap and using your rolling pin as a support, drape it over the cake. Smooth the marzipan into position with the palm of your hand working from the centre to the edge and down the sides. Trim away any excess marzipan with a sharp knife. Use the remaining apricot jam to brush over the marzipan to ensure that the icing sticks to the cake. Colour about 750 g (1 lb 10 oz) of ready-to-roll icing pink using a few drops of pink food colouring and roll out to form a large circle about 45 cm (18 in) diameter – again, this is best done on top of the plastic wrap. Cut the circumference of the circle in a fairly free wavy pattern. Drape the icing over the cake so that it is smooth at the top but then hangs down in folds to form the skirt.

TO MAKE UP THE ICING TO PIPE AROUND THE DRESS, beat a small egg white until stiff then gently beat in about 200 g (7 oz) icing sugar with a squeeze of lemon to get a fairly stiff mixture. Pipe this icing in two layers around the dress to form the ruching and decorate with the iced flowers. Take some of the remaining ready-to-roll icing and roll this out thinly on to a surface dredged with sifted icing sugar and cut into petal shapes. Remove the swirls of icing from the gem biscuits. Decorate the cake with the icing petals, edible gold balls and swirls of icing from the gem biscuits as in the photograph. Using a sharp knife, cut a hole in the centre of the cake, remove the inside and place the doll (appropriately dressed) in the centre of the cake.

TO ADD THE FINISHING TOUCH, make a hat for the fairy princess by attaching a pink Party Ring biscuit at a jaunty angle on the doll's head with a little of the piped icing, place an iced gem biscuit in the centre and decorate with a feather. You can add edible gold balls for earrings and give the doll an umbrella to hold.

Fairy Tale Castle Cake

N

3 Madeira cakes

5 tbsp apricot jam

2 large and 1 small Swiss rolls

6 ice-cream cones

PINK BUTTER ICING

225 g (8 oz) unsalted butter

450 g (1 lb) icing sugar, sifted

35 ml (7 tsp) milk

few drops of pink food
   colouring

WHITE ICING

100 g (4 oz) unsalted butter

225 g (8 oz) sifted icing sugar

20 ml (4 tsp) milk

Decoration ingredients are
   given overleaf

This birthday cake only needs assembling and decorating since it is made with bought Madeira cakes and Swiss rolls. It looks fabulous and if you follow the instructions carefully you can't go wrong.

Trim the Madeira cakes if necessary so that you end up with a level block. Warm and sieve the apricot jam. Stick the Madeira cakes in the centre of a 32 cm (12½ in) square cake board by brushing the base of the cakes with a little of the apricot jam. To make a pink butter icing of spreading consistency, cream together the butter and icing sugar and beat in the milk and pink food colouring. Cover the surface of the cake with the icing and smooth evenly with a palette knife. Cut each of the Swiss rolls in half and cover the sides of these with the pink butter icing. Place the two smaller Swiss roll halves on top of the Madeira cake in the front two corners and place two of the large halves on the two back corners. Place the two remaining large halves on either side of the castle at the back and secure them to the cake board with a little apricot jam.

TO MAKE A WHITE ICING of spreading consistency, cream together the butter, icing sugar and milk. Cover the six ice-cream cones with the white icing using a palette knife. Attach

DECORATION

ice-cream wafers

coloured miniature
    marshmallows

iced gem biscuits

3 pink wafer sandwiches

chocolate sticks

75 g (3 oz) desiccated coconut

blue food colouring

white royal icing (see page 62)

1 large egg white

200 g (7 oz) icing sugar or
    writing icing

the cones to form turrets, either using some icing or – if you want the castle to be more secure– stick a fairly long bamboo skewer through each of the Swiss rolls. You can then rest the ice-cream cones on each of these.

CUT THE WAFERS CAREFULLY with a serrated edge knife to make the windows of the castle and press these on to the Swiss rolls. Decorate the turrets with miniature marshmallows and the base of the castle with iced gem biscuits. Make a drawbridge from two-and-a-half pink wafer sandwiches and cut some chocolate sticks down to size to form the portcullis.

TO MAKE THE WHITE ROYAL ICING for piping the windows, beat the egg white and gradually add the sifted icing sugar, beating until the icing is smooth (add more or less icing sugar to make the right consistency for piping). Alternatively, to save time you can buy tubes of writing icing with piping nozzles. Using a small star nozzle, pipe little rosettes around the wafer windows and decorate the drawbridge. To create the moat around the castle, mix the desiccated coconut with a few drops of the blue food colouring and a few drops of water. Brush the cake board with some warm, sieved apricot jam and strew the coconut over the cake board.

Swimming Pool Cake

This cake may take a little more time than the others in this book but it is actually not difficult to make and it will certainly make the children want to dive in.

Brush a 30 x 20 cm (12 x 8 in) cake board (or use a slightly larger cake board if you wish) with some warmed apricot jam and position one of the cakes on the board. Cut a 12.5 x 20 cm (5 x 8 in) rectangle from the centre of the second cake.

To make the buttercream, beat together the butter, sifted icing sugar, orange rind and juice until smooth. Spread a thin layer of buttercream over the top of the first cake and place the cake 'frame' on top. Reserve a little of the buttercream and use a palette knife, to cover the cake with the remainder.

To make the swimming pool, use the Belgian chocolate for the surround, cutting it with a long serrated knife in a seesaw action to fit. Then sift the icing sugar into a bowl and beat together with the egg whites or use water until thick and then colour blue. Reserve a little of the blue icing and spoon or pipe the remainder into the centre of the pool, but leave about 2.5 cm (1 in) of the inside edge of the pool above the water line and spread this with a thin layer of buttercream.

❄ sponge cake only

two 30 x 20 cm (12 x 8 in)
   sponge cakes (see Three
   Bears' Cake on page 98)
2 tbsp apricot jam

ORANGE BUTTERCREAM

225 g (8 oz) butter, softened
450 g (1 lb) sifted icing sugar
1 orange, grated rind and juice

SWIMMING POOL

400 g (14 oz) white luxury
   Belgian chocolate
350 g (12 oz) icing sugar
2 egg whites or 45 ml (3 tbsp)
   water
blue, pink, brown, yellow and
   red edible food colouring
   pastes
8 pink wafer biscuits
coloured sweets
2 red liquorice laces

HALVE FIVE PINK WAFERS LENGTHWAYS and stick around the inside edge of the pool. Arrange a layer of coloured sweets above. Use a teaspoon to pull the blue icing to the sides of the pool to look like ripples and make waves on the water's surface. Use the reserved blue icing to make small puddles on the swimming pool surround: these are great for hiding any joins in the chocolate.

MAKE A DIVING BOARD from a small square off-cut from the leftover cake. Stick to the side of the pool with buttercream and cover the top and sides with a thin layer of buttercream. Cover the three sides with halved wafers, cut to fit, and put two whole pink wafers on top. Arrange the liquorice laces to form the handles of the steps down to the pool.

FOR THE BATHERS, cut the ready-to-roll icing in half and colour one half a pinky flesh colour. Form into the faces, bodies and limbs of the swimmers. Colour a little of the icing blue and roll on a lightly floured surface and cut to form bathing trunks and a bathing costume. Colour a little red and form into a bathing suit, arm bands and a towel. Colour a little brown and push through a garlic press to make hair. Stick on to the bathers' heads and draw features with icing pens. Colour a little yellow and form into the rubber rings. Assemble the bathers and position as shown in the photograph. Decorate the rubber ring with red spots using a writing icing pen and place on top of the towel by the side of the pool.

BATHERS

1 x 500 g (1 lb 2 oz) packet ready-to-roll white icing
black and red writing icing pens or use tubes of writing icing

Burger and Chips

MAKES 10 BURGER AND CHIP MEALS

900 g (2 lb) ready-to-roll
white icing
green and red edible food
colouring paste
aluminium foil

BURGERS
3 x 65 g (2½ oz) Mars Bars
25 g (1 oz) plain chocolate
75 g (3 oz) butter
100 g (4 oz) Rice Krispies

Decoration ingredients are
given overleaf

You would have to look twice at this to realise that it is not the real thing! I noticed that at many parties my children attended, a squashed, soggy slice of birthday cake would come back home wrapped in a paper napkin in the party bag. I thought it would be a good idea if the cake wasn't going to be eaten at the party to make really fun looking individual birthday cakes that the children could take home with them in a little box. These cakes are easy to make and I'm sure older children will love to give you a helping hand.

Make the lettuce leaves first so that they can be moulded into shape and left to harden. Cut off 250 g (9 oz) of the ready-to-roll icing and knead in enough green food colouring to turn it pale green. Roll this out into about ten thin circles, each approximately 7.5 cm (3 in) in diameter with slightly uneven edges. To make the veins of the lettuce, dip a cocktail stick into some cornflour and press lightly while rolling it over the icing. Frill the edges of the lettuce by rolling a cocktail stick dipped in cornflour backwards and forwards. Lightly scrumple up ten pieces of aluminium foil and form each into a circle a little smaller than the lettuce leaves. Lay the green icing over the foil, press down lightly and allow to harden overnight.

DECORATION

tubes of black and yellow
    writing icing
10 tsp redcurrant jelly
3 tbsp sesame seeds
10 doughnuts (about 7.5 cm/
    3 in diameter)
10 paper plates
10 red paper cups
greaseproof paper
4 x 150 g (5 oz) packets white
    chocolate fingers

TO MAKE THE BURGERS, cut the Mars Bars into pieces, put them into a large saucepan together with the chocolate and butter and melt over a low heat, stirring occasionally. Stir in the Rice Krispies until they are well coated. To make the round hamburger shapes, take a 7.5 cm (3 in) pastry cutter and place it on a large non-stick baking tray. Spoon the Rice Krispie mixture into the round pastry cutter to a depth of about 5 mm (¼ in) and press down with a teaspoon to level the surface. Carefully remove the pastry cutter and repeat with the remaining Rice Krispie mixture to make ten burger shapes and put these in the fridge to set.

FOR THE BURGER FILLING, cut off 250 g (9 oz) of the ready-to-roll icing and colour it red by kneading in some edible red food colouring. Roll out to a thickness of about 5 mm (¼ in) and cut into ten circles using a 5 cm (2 in) pastry cutter. Cut each circle in half and use the black writing icing to make little dots of black to resemble the tomato seeds. Cut a slice off the remaining white icing and form into 20 thin slices of onion.

THE TOMATO KETCHUP CONTAINERS are made from the remainder of the white icing formed into ten small rectangular containers. Fill each of these with 1 tsp redcurrant jelly. Add a foil cover, which you can roll back a little to expose the 'ketchup'. Toast the sesame seeds in a dry frying pan until lightly golden.

TO ASSEMBLE EACH BURGER, cut a doughnut in half horizontally and put one half on a paper plate. Place the Rice Krispie burger on one half, arrange a slice of tomatoes and two onion slices on top and pipe on a little yellow icing for mustard. Then add a lettuce leaf and place the other half of the doughnut on top and sprinkle with a few of the toasted sesame seeds. Finish off with a few little squirts of the yellow writing icing for mustard. Cut about one-third off the height of each red paper cup and cut a V-shape out of the centre. Crumple some greaseproof paper in the base of the cup and arrange about nine white chocolate fingers in the cup to look like chips.

PRESENT EACH CHILD with a meal consisting of burger in a bun, chips and ketchup. place on a paper plate and cover with foil for transporting or pack into small boxes.

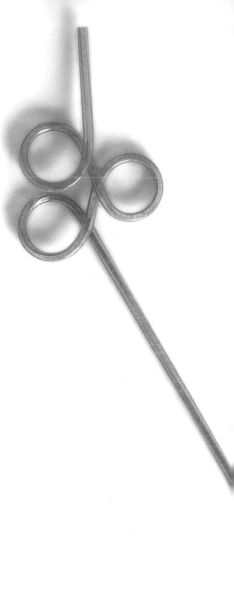

Cat with Kittens

575 g (1 lb 4oz) ready-to-roll
  white icing
1 tbsp apricot jam
variety of food colour pens
  (optional)

CAT, KITTENS AND MOUSE
1 large chocolate Swiss roll
1 quantity chocolate
  buttercream (see page 60)
1 tube black writing icing
2 green Smarties
6 chocolate buttons
1 pink Smartie
red liquorice laces
1 Matchmaker chocolate stick
3 mini-Swiss rolls
4 green mini-Smarties
2 brown mini-Smarties
birthday candles
blue food colouring
red food colouring
pink food colouring
2 edible silver balls

The beauty of this cake is that it is very quick to make and there is no baking involved.

Roll out 500 g (1 lb) of the icing into a circle to fit a 30 cm (12 in) cake board. Brush the board with the warmed apricot jam. Cover the board with the icing and trim the edges. If you like, you can decorate the icing with coloured sugar art pens.

FOR THE CAT, cut off a quarter length from the large Swiss roll and attach it on top of the remainder with chocolate buttercream. Roll out some of the white icing and cut out two circles for eyes. Attach to the face with chocolate buttercream. With black writing icing draw a line down the centre of each green Smartie and stick in the centre of the white circles. Using chocolate buttons, the pink Smartie and red liquorice laces make the face as in the photograph. Use a Matchmaker for the tail. For the kittens, use two mini-Swiss rolls for the bodies. Cut 3 cm (1¼ in) off the ends of the third mini-Swiss roll for the heads and attach with chocolate buttercream. Make their faces as opposite (with mini-Smarties) and insert candles for tails.

FOR THE BOWL, colour half the remaining white icing blue and mould into shape. Add a white circle of icing as milk. Colour the rest pale pink, mould into the shape of a mouse and add silver balls for eyes. Make a ball of wool from the liquorice laces.

Special Occasion Parties

Mother's Day Breakfast

This is always on a Sunday so it is a perfect opportunity for children to do something really special for their mother – or father on Father's Day. Children will adore to present their mum or dad with an indulgent breakfast in bed. For young children, mum can help out on Father's Day and dad can lend a hand on Mother's Day. If dad is partial to a cooked breakfast, you could help your child prepare the heart-shaped egg on page 122 and serve it with bacon or sausages.

Apart from the recipes themselves you can go to town on the presentation. Lay a pretty napkin over a tray and maybe put a single rose in a small vase. Perhaps write and design a breakfast menu and don't forget to include your mum or dad's favourite newspaper or magazine and a nice cup of tea or coffee. Post a note on the fridge door the night before telling mum or dad to have a lie-in the following morning and to expect breakfast in bed. Alternatively, make it a big surprise – but you will need to get out of bed early!

Perfect Pancakes

Pancakes for breakfast are a real treat and you can make delicious, really thin pancakes with this foolproof batter. Sprinkle them with lemon juice and dust with icing sugar or serve with maple syrup and perhaps some fresh fruit.

MAKES 12 PANCAKES

100 g (4 oz) plain flour

a generous pinch of salt

1 egg

300 ml (½ pint) milk

50 g (2 oz) melted butter

Sift the flour with a big pinch of salt into a mixing bowl, make a well in the centre and add the egg. Use a balloon whisk to incorporate the eggs into the flour and gradually whisk in the milk. Stir the mixture until smooth but do not overmix.

TO MAKE THE PANCAKES, use a heavy bottomed 15-18 cm (6-7 in) frying pan and brush with the melted butter (either use a pastry brush or dip some crumpled kitchen towel into the butter to coat the base of the pan) and when hot, pour in about 30 ml (2 tbsp) of the batter. Quickly tilt the pan from side to side until you get a thin layer of batter covering the base of the frying pan. Cook the pancake for about 1 minute, then flip it over (you can use a spatula for this) and cook until the underside is lightly flecked with gold. Continue with the rest of the batter, brushing the pan with melted butter when necessary.

ANY PANCAKES YOU DON'T USE can be frozen, interleaved with non-stick paper and wrapped in a freezer bag.

Fruit Salad with Honey Yoghurt Dressing

Fresh fruit presented in a slightly different way makes a great treat for mum. Make a fruit salad using seasonal fruits and top with a mixture of Greek yoghurt and honey. Alternatively, make a fruit plate and serve with a bowl of yoghurt and honey for dipping.

Mango, Strawberry and Banana Fruit Smoothie

MAKES 1 TALL OR 2 SMALL GLASSES

3 strawberries

100 g (4 oz) peeled and
chopped mango flesh

1 small or ½ medium banana

1 orange, squeezed

1 passion fruit (optional)

This is especially good when sweet juicy mangoes are in season. You could also make this using a fresh juicy peach instead of banana when peaches are in season.

Wash and hull the strawberries and then simply blend all the fruit together.

Apple and Carrot Breakfast Muffins

Here is a healthy and deliciously moist muffin that's bound to become a family favourite. These muffins are very easy to make and will keep well for up to five days.

Pre-heat the oven to 180°C/350°F/Gas 4. Combine the flour, sugar, skimmed milk powder, baking powder, cinnamon, salt and ginger in a mixing bowl. In a separate bowl, combine the oil, honey, maple syrup, eggs and vanilla essence. Beat lightly with a wire whisk until blended. Add the grated apple, carrots and raisins to the liquid mixture and stir well. Fold in the dry ingredients until just combined but don't over mix or the muffins will become heavy. Line a muffin tray with paper cups and fill the muffin cups until two-thirds full. Bake for 20 to 25 minutes.

MAKES 12 MUFFINS

150 g (5 oz) plain wholemeal flour

50 g (2 oz) granulated sugar

25 g (1 oz) dried skimmed milk powder

1½ tsp baking powder

½ tsp cinnamon

¼ tsp salt

¼ tsp ginger

125 ml (4 fl oz) vegetable oil

4 tbsp honey

4 tbsp maple syrup

2 eggs, lightly beaten

½ tsp vanilla essence

1 large apple, peeled and grated

75 g (3 oz) carrots, peeled and grated

65 g (2½ oz) raisins

A Hearty Breakfast

This heart-shaped egg would make a fun surprise breakfast for mum or dad and only takes a few minutes to prepare. It would be fun also to pipe mummy or daddy's name on the plate using some tomato ketchup – this can be done using a piping bag with a thin nozzle or you can make your own throw-away piping bag by rolling up a small piece of greaseproof paper. Older children will enjoy helping you make this – it is also good served with baked beans for a hearty breakfast.

MAKES 1 PORTION

1 thick slice white bread

15 g (½ oz) butter plus an
    extra knob

1 egg

salt and freshly ground black
    pepper

Cut a hole in the centre of the bread using a heart-shaped cookie cutter approximately 8 cm (3 in) wide at its widest point. Melt the butter in a small frying pan and sauté the bread on one side until golden. Turn the bread over, melt an extra knob of butter in the heart-shaped cut-out, break the egg into it and season lightly. Cook covered for about 2 minutes or until the egg is cooked to your liking. You can also dip the cut out heart in a little egg and sauté that too to make French bread.

Mock-fried Egg

MAKES 1

1 small carton vanilla or
  natural yoghurt
1 canned peach half

You would have to look closely at this to see that this is a no-cholesterol version of a fried egg!

Carefully spoon the yoghurt into a coloured bowl or plate and then place the rounded half of a canned peach in the centre to look like the yolk.

Fruity Swiss-style Muesli

This healthy, delicious cereal makes a welcome alternative to the sugary over-processed cereals designed for children nowadays. It was invented by the famous Swiss physician Dr Bircher-Benner to give his patients a healthy, well-rounded breakfast. You can add many different fruits like peaches or strawberries and instead of oats and wheatgerm, you could use a muesli base made from wheat, barley and rye flakes, porridge oats and jumbo oats, which you can often buy in health food stores.

Soak the oats and wheatgerm in the juice for about 10 minutes or you could soak them overnight. Sprinkle the lemon juice over the grated apple and then simply combine all the ingredients.

MAKES 4 PORTIONS

N

75 g (3 oz) rolled oats

40 g (1½ oz) toasted wheatgerm

250 ml (8 fl oz) apple juice or apple and mango juice

2 tsp lemon juice

1 large apple, peeled and grated

1 small orange, cut into segments with the pith removed

8 grapes (preferably black), halved and de-seeded

50 g (2 oz) dried apricots, chopped

2 tbsp raisins

2 tsp honey

2 tbsp finely chopped hazelnuts (optional)

Easter

EASTER PARTY INVITATIONS
You will need: stiff coloured
card, coloured paper, gold pen
(optional), coloured ribbons
Cut stiff coloured card into the
shape of an egg and decorate
with triangles and strips of
coloured paper and maybe a
gold pen. Write the party
details on the back and tie a
ribbon with a bow around the
middle.

Children love nothing better than a traditional egg hunt. For older children this can involve clues; for younger children, hide the eggs in the garden if the weather is good or around the house. Decorating hard-boiled eggs with paints and glitter or making egg people (see page 131) will keep children amused.

Easter is a chocaholics dream but all too often there is a glut of Easter eggs, so here are a few ideas if you do have surplus stock. Break up hollow Easter eggs to make chocolate chips for use in recipes like Coconut Kisses (page 69) or melt them as in Divinely Decadent Dark Chocolate and Apricot Bars (page 71). Alternatively, make a fruit fondue, melting chocolate and keeping it warm to use as a dip for a selection of fruits like strawberries, pineapple or grapes.

Easter Games

As well as the games features on pages 18-26 there are some great games specifically to play at Easter.

Easter Egg Hunt

Props: chocolate Easter eggs, baskets or bags
Hide lots of little chocolate Easter eggs around the house or in the garden. Give each child a bag or a

basket and let them search and collect as many eggs as they can find. You can give children various tasks like find 8 eggs wrapped in different colours or find 2 wrapped in gold, 2 wrapped in silver and 2 spotted eggs. The winner could get a very special Easter egg as a prize.

Pass the Egg

Props: spoons, chocolate eggs

Divide the children into two teams. Each child holds a spoon in his mouth with the aim of passing a chocolate egg from spoon to spoon without it dropping. If the egg falls on the floor, it has to be picked up with a spoon still held in the mouth.

Spoof!

Props: mini-chocolate Easter eggs

Give each child three small Easter eggs and sit them in a circle. When someone calls 'Spoof!', the children have to choose to put none, one, two or three Easter eggs in their right hand without letting anyone else see how many they have. They should hide their other hand behind their back. The children then take it in turns to guess the total number of eggs in the children's right hands. For example, if there are six children there could be as many as 36 eggs. Note down the numbers and no one is allowed to guess the same number as another child. When the children open up their fists, the child who is farthest away from the correct total is out.

Easter Chocolate Nest

👨‍🍳 ❄️ without the decoration

CHOCOLATE CAKE

175 g (6 oz) plain flour

50 g (2 oz) cocoa powder

1 tsp baking powder

1 tsp bicarbonate of soda

4 tbsp golden syrup

2 eggs

150 ml (5 fl oz) milk

150 ml (5 fl oz) sunflower oil

2 tbsp apricot jam

200 g (7 oz) milk chocolate

100 ml (3 fl oz) double cream

25 g (1 oz) butter

½ tsp grated orange zest

DECORATION

5 chocolate flake bars

chocolate eggs

It is easy to transform this delicious chocolate cake into a special Easter celebration cake with some chocolate flake bars and mini-Easter eggs.

Pre-heat the oven to 170°C/325°F/Gas 3. Sieve the flour, cocoa powder, baking powder and bicarbonate of soda into a mixing bowl. Beat in the remaining cake ingredients. Divide the mixture between two 20 cm (8 in) round sandwich cake tins. Bake in the oven for 20 to 25 minutes or until a skewer inserted in the centre of the cake comes out clean.

Allow the cakes to cool in their tins, then turn out on to a cooling rack. When cool, sandwich together with apricot jam.

TO MAKE THE CHOCOLATE ICING, put the milk chocolate and cream in a heatproof bowl over a pan of simmering water. Stir until the chocolate has melted, remove from the heat and beat in the butter. Add the orange rind. Put the icing in the fridge for about 30 minutes to set a little and then spread over the top and sides of the cake. Decorate with chocolate flakes and Easter eggs to make a nest.

Easter Biscuits

MAKES 20 BISCUITS

100 g (4 oz) softened butter

75 g (3 oz) caster sugar

1 egg, separated

200 g (7 oz) plain flour

pinch of salt

½ tsp mixed spice

½ tsp ground cinnamon

50 g (2 oz) currants

25 g (1 oz) mixed peel, finely chopped

1½ tbsp milk

Children will enjoy rolling out these traditional Easter biscuits and cutting them into shapes.

Pre-heat the oven to 200°C/400°F/Gas 6. Put the butter and sugar into a bowl and cream together until light and fluffy. Beat in the egg yolk and reserve the egg white. Sift together the flour, salt, mixed spice and cinnamon and mix into the creamed butter and sugar. Add the currants, mixed peel and milk.

Lightly flour a clean work surface and knead the mixture until it forms a soft dough. Roll out to a thickness of about 5 mm (¼ in). Cut into rounds using a 7 cm (2¾ in) fluted cutter. Knead and re-roll trimmings to cut out more rounds until all the dough is used up. Place on greased or lined baking trays.

BAKE FOR 8 TO 10 MINUTES, then remove from the oven, brush the biscuits with lightly beaten egg white and sprinkle with a little caster sugar and return to the oven for 4 to 5 minutes, or until the biscuits are lightly golden. Lift on to a wire rack to cool and store in an airtight container.

Egg People

A fun activity for children at Easter is to decorate hard-boiled eggs. Make hats from egg cartons, empty toilet rolls and odds and ends like feathers, cotton wool, lace and ribbon. You can make plaits from wool and paint faces on the eggs with black and red felt pens.

Easter Bonnet Cakes

These are easy to make and look fabulous. You can colour the icing using a few drops of edible food colouring to make different coloured hats.

Pre-heat the oven to 180°C/350°F/Gas 4. Cream together the butter and sugar until light and fluffy. Add an egg at a time with 1 tablespoon of the flour. Fold in the remaining flour together with the milk, lemon rind and vanilla essence.

Grease and flour two 27 x 18 cm (11 x 7 in) shallow baking tins. Spread the mixture evenly over the base of the tins and bake for 20 minutes (a skewer inserted in the centre of the cake will come out clean when the cake is ready).

TO MAKE THE BONNETS, cut each sponge into six circles using a 7.5 cm (3 in) round cutter. Stick a marshmallow in the centre of each circle using warmed apricot jam. Roll out 50 g (2 oz) of icing at a time and cut into circles about 2.5-4 cm (1-1½ in) wider all the way round than the cake. Brush the marshmallows and cake bases with warmed apricot jam and lay the circles of icing over the centres. Mould to the shapes of the cakes and trim away any excess icing. Tie liquorice laces in a bow around the base of the marshmallows and decorate with sugar flowers, attached to the icing with a little of the warmed apricot jam.

MAKES 12 EASTER BONNET CAKES

175 g (6 oz) butter

175 g (6 oz) caster sugar

3 eggs

175 g (6 oz) self-raising flour

1 tbsp milk

½ tsp grated lemon rind

1 tsp vanilla essence

4 tbsp apricot jam

12 marshmallows

600 g (1 lb 5 oz) ready-to-roll white icing

DECORATION

red and green liquorice laces

sugar flowers

Teddy Bear's Picnic

TEDDY BEAR'S PICNIC INVITATION
You will need: coloured sheets of A4 paper, sticky tape, envelopes, pencil, felt pens Take two sheets of A4 paper. Fold each sheet in half to make it A5 size and then fold in half again so that it is 7.5 cm (3 in) wide. Draw a teddy bear on the paper about 12 cm (5 in) tall with the teddy bear's arms quite wide and stretching right to the edges of the paper. Cut around the outline of the teddy bear, but do not cut around the folded edges. Unfold the bears and stick together the two strips of paper with Sellotape and you will have eight teddy bears holding hands. Draw faces on the teddy bears and write the part details on the back.

Teddy bear picnics are fun, particularly in the summer when you can hold them outdoors. You don't even have to venture far as it can be just as much fun in your own back garden. However, always have an alternative indoor venue if the weather turns against you – even if it is only a large rug on the kitchen floor.

Adding to the Fun

- Ask each child to bring along a favourite teddy bear.
- As a fun activity get the children to make up Edible Necklaces (page 141) when they arrive, which they can either wear around their necks or adorn their teddy bears with.
- Make up the picnic so that you can give each child an individual box of food containing sandwiches, cakes, fruit, etc.
- After the picnic, make up clues so the children can go on a treasure hunt for the 'honeypot' filled with lots of goodies.
- Wash fruit thoroughly before packing it up for the picnic so that it is ready to eat. as soon as you get there.

Teddy Bear's Picnic Games

As well as the games features on pages 18-26 here are some ideas for games to play at a Teddy Bear's Picnic.

Treasure Hunt

Props: cream paper, matches, pen

Before the picnic, write and hide clues. Give out the first clue, which will lead to the second, third and eventually the treasure. It is fun to write the clues on sheets of paper that have been singed around the edges with a match and then rolled up and tied with string. Another way to hide clues is to write them on a small piece of paper, insert them into a balloon, then blow up the balloon and hide it. To read the clue, the children will first have to burst the balloon.

'Teddy says ...'

Props: one teddy bear

Holding a teddy, stand in front of the children and make up actions like, 'Teddy says hop on one foot' and all the children have to hop on one foot until he decides to change the action to something like, 'Teddy says touch your nose with your foot'. The catch is that the action must be prefixed by 'Teddy says' for them to follow orders. If he says, 'Go on all fours and bark like a dog', the children should not follow because teddy didn't say so. Any child who does the action by mistake is then out. The game continues until only one child is left.

WHAT TO TAKE ON A PICNIC

A plastic sheet to put on the ground.

Rugs to sit on.

Plenty of paper napkins or kitchen towels and maybe some wet wipes.

Ice packs and an insulated bag for keeping drinks and food cold.

Paper plates and plastic cups.

Plastic cartons for transporting salads and sandwiches, etc.

Some large plastic bin liners to put all the rubbish in.

Leafy green salads should be packed separately from the dressing so they don't go mushy

Small prizes for the games.

Salad on a Stick

MAKES AS MANY AS YOU LIKE

cubes or slices of cheese

chunks of cucumber and carrot

cherry tomatoes

slices of turkey

seedless grapes

chunks of pineapple

slices of kiwi

strawberries

dried apricots

Serve a variety of healthy foods on a kebab or cocktail stick. Make savoury kebabs or fruit kebabs using any of the suggestions given here.

Teddy Bear Sandwiches

It's fun to make sandwiches cut into teddy bear shapes using cookie cutters. Choose some popular fillings for the sandwiches like peanut butter, egg mayonnaise, cream cheese, Marmite or strawberry jam. If you can find teddy bear cookie cutters in varying sizes you could even make a family of teddy bears.

Chocolate Orange Mini-muffins

Mini muffins are just the right size for small children and these are really easy and quick to make. The combination of chocolate with a hint of orange is irresistible.

Pre-heat the oven to 180°C/350°F/Gas 4. Cream together the margarine and caster sugar. Sift together the flour and cocoa. Add the eggs to the creamed mixture, a little at a time, together with 1 tablespoon of the flour mixture.

   Fold in the remaining flour and cocoa until blended. Stir in the orange rind and chocolate chips. Line some muffin trays with paper cases and two-thirds fill each of the cases. Transfer to the pre-heated oven and cook for 12 to 15 minutes. When cool, you can sieve some icing sugar over the muffins for decoration.

ALTERNATIVELY, decorate to look like teddy bears using chocolate buttons for ears, mini Smarties for eyes and melted chocolate.

MAKES 30 MINI-MUFFINS OR 15 MEDIUM MUFFINS

🎅 ❄ without the decoration

100 g (4 oz) soft margarine

100 g (4 oz) caster sugar

100 g (4 oz) self-raising flour

2 tbsp cocoa powder

2 eggs, lightly beaten

grated rind of 1 small orange

50 g (2 oz) chocolate chips

a little icing sugar (optional)

DECORATION

chocolate buttons

mini Smarties

melted chocolate

OVERLEAF
Teddy Bear Sandwiches (see left)
Chocolate Orange Mini-muffins
(see above)
Teddy Bear Biscuits (p140)

Teddy Bear Biscuits

MAKES 20 BISCUITS

👨‍🍳 ❄ without the decoration

100 g (4 oz) butter at room
    temperature
50 g (2 oz) caster sugar
175 g (6 oz) plain flour
pinch of salt
a few drops of vanilla essence

DECORATION
edible silver balls
currants
glacé icing (see page 62)
pink and blue food colouring

Children love these teddy bear shaped biscuits and they are easy and quick to make. I have various size teddy bear biscuit cutters so I can make a whole family of teddy bears.

Pre-heat the oven to 180°C/350°F/Gas 4. Beat the butter and sugar together either by hand with a wooden spoon or in an electric mixer. Sift together the flour and salt and mix this into the butter mixture together with a few drops of vanilla essence to form a fairly stiff dough. If the dough is too dry, add a little water. Form the dough into a ball, then roll out thinly on a floured work surface using a rolling pin dusted with flour. Cut into teddy shapes using biscuit cutters. Collect all the trimmings together and roll these out again to make more biscuits. Add edible silver balls or currants for eyes before baking. Bake for about 15 minutes or until the biscuits are lightly golden. Cool the biscuits on a wire rack.

MAKE UP ONE QUANTITY OF THE GLACÉ ICING and colour one half pink and one half pale blue. Pipe clothes on to the teddy bears using the icing and decorate some of the girl teddies with sugar flowers. Alternatively, leave the teddy bears plain and tie bows of thin ribbon around their necks.

Edible Necklaces

Making necklaces using an assortment of non-messy foods is great fun for children. Use a large, fairly blunt needle and choose from the foods listed below to design your own necklace on a length of wool or use licquorice laces. A good way to encourage your child to eat healthy foods is to thread two or three treats on to the necklace so that your child has to eat the healthy foods before reaching the treats.

wool or liquorice laces

HEALTHY FOODS

miniature cheeses

chunks of cucumber, carrot, celery or sweet pepper

cherry tomatoes

dried apricots and apple rings

· dates

breakfast cereals with a hole in the middle

round pretzels

black and white grapes

TREATS

Liquorice Allsorts

marshmallows

Polos

wine gums

biscuits with a hole in the middle

Hula Hoops

Coronation Chicken

MAKES 6 PORTIONS

2 chicken breasts, cut into
 bite-sized chunks

½ chicken stock cube

1 bay leaf

15 ml (1 tbsp) vegetable oil

1 small onion, finely chopped

1 tsp medium curry powder

1½ tbsp mango chutney

1½ tbsp lemon juice

1½ tbsp tomato purée

150 ml (5 fl oz) mayonnaise

75 ml (2½ fl oz) mild natural
 yoghurt

Coronation chicken has a delicious flavour and will keep for several days in the fridge. It can be served as a salad with rice. It also makes a good sandwich filling with some crisp lettuce between the slices of bread or is good with lettuce and cucumber rolled up inside a mini-tortilla or in a pitta pocket.

Dissolve the chicken stock cube in 10 fl oz (½ pint) water and put into a saucepan together with the bay leaf. Bring to the boil then reduce the heat and poach the chicken for about 6 minutes. Leave the chicken in the stock to cool down.

FOR THE SAUCE, heat the oil in a pan, add the chopped onion and sauté for 2 minutes. Stir in the curry powder and cook for 30 seconds. Stir in the mango chutney, lemon juice, tomato purée and 75 ml (2½ fl oz) of the chicken stock. Simmer for 10 minutes. Strain through a sieve and allow to cool. Mix together with the mayonnaise and the yoghurt. Mix in the chicken and fruit if using.

Chicken Salad

This is a delicious, easy-to-prepare chicken salad. You could also substitute flaked tuna for the chicken if you like.

Poach the chicken for 10 minutes in the stock, then leave to cool completely. Then remove the chicken with a slotted spoon. This can be prepared the night before. To make the dressing, whisk together all of the ingredients (or use a hand blender). Mix together all of the salad ingredients and toss in the dressing.

MAKES 6 PORTIONS

600 ml (1 pint) chicken stock

2 small chicken breasts, cut into bite-sized pieces

100 g (4 oz) pasta shapes, cooked and cooled

100 g (4 oz) canned or cooked frozen sweetcorn

18 small cherry tomatoes, cut in half

2 spring onions, finely sliced

½ baby gem lettuce, shredded

DRESSING

3 tbsp olive oil

1 tbsp white wine vinegar

½ tsp Dijon mustard

½ tsp sugar

salt and freshly ground pepper

1 tbsp chicken stock from the poaching liquid

Summer Barbecue

PICNIC HAMPER INVITATION
You will need: coloured paper, glue, felt pens.

Make a picnic basket using yellow paper and glue and decorate with a black felt pen, then write the details of the party on a 'paper plate' cut-out and put this into the picnic basket together with several other paper cut-outs of food and drink.

Summer barbecues are wonderful. Organise any of the outdoor games from pages 25-26 and make sure that children are well away from the barbecue so that they don't get burnt. Lighting the barbecue can be a trying time, so if you find charcoal briquettes difficult to light, try using a bag of easy light charcoal. If is especially useful for a party as you don't need to handle the charcoal. Just place the bag in position and light.

To further ensure a smooth-running party, plan the order in which you barbecue food so that the various foods receive the correct cooking time. For example, barbecue fish skewers last as they will only need a few minutes.

Adding to the Fun

- Try not to pack food too tightly on to a skewer as it is important that you leave some gaps so that the food can be cooked thoroughly.
- Brush the cooking rack with a little oil before barbecuing. This will help prevent the food from sticking.
- To avoid flare-ups, trim excess fat from meat and do not add too much oil to marinades.
- If the marinade has a high sugar content, try to scrape most of the marinade off the food before grilling and baste the food during the last 10 minutes, otherwise it tends to burn.
- Soak wooden kebab sticks in cold water for at least 30 minutes before use to prevent them scorching.
- Keep raw and cooked food separate.
- If using a charcoal barbecue, allow at least 45 minutes for it to reach the correct temperature. Only start cooking when all the flames have died down and the coals are glowing red under a thin coating of grey ash. A gas barbecue will probably be ready in 10 minutes.
- Sear the food quite close to the hot coals to seal in the juices and give a distinctive barbecue taste, then move the food further away from the coals to finish cooking.
- A hinged wire rack is ideal for barbecuing hamburgers, pieces of fish or vegetables and makes turning foods easy.
- Most foods that are suitable for barbecuing can also be cooked indoors under the grill if the weather turns.
- Children also like lamb cutlets brushed with a little ketchup and oil on the barbecue and if you don't want to cook too much, hot dogs and warmed pitta bread will always go down a treat..
- Children will enjoy toasting marshmallows on long forks or skewers over the barbecue.

Barbecue Jacket Potatoes

baking potatoes
vegetable oil
butter
sour cream
chives
salt and freshly ground black
   pepper

Wash and dry the potatoes, prick the skins several times and brush with vegetable oil. Either place directly on the grill or wrap each potato in foil and cook for 45 to 60 minutes, turning occasionally, depending on the size of the potato. They are delicious if you scoop out the flesh, leaving a shell, and mash this together with some butter, sour cream, snipped chives and seasoning. Spoon the mixture back into the shell and heat through on the barbecue.

Corn-on-the-cob

SERVES 4

4 corn-on-the-cobs
15 g (½ oz) butter, softened
salt and freshly ground black
   pepper

Remove the corn husks and rinse well. Place each cob on a sheet of extra thick aluminium foil. Brush all over with the softened butter. Season with salt and pepper and sprinkle with water. Fold over the foil to make a snug package. Place on the barbecue and grill for about 20 minutes or until the corn is tender, turning several times. Unwrap the corn, taking care as it will be very hot, and barbecue for a couple of minutes turning occasionally to get a slightly charred effect. For young children it is best to cut the cobs in half before they are barbecued.

Chicken Satay Sticks

These are a great treat for peanut butter lovers. They are delicious on their own or can be dipped into a scrumptious peanut sauce.

Mix together all the ingredients for the marinade and marinate the cubes of chicken for at least 1 hour. Soak eight bamboo skewers in water for at least 30 minutes to prevent them from scorching under the grill. Thread the chicken on to the skewers, leaving a small gap between each piece and barbecue for about 7 minutes, turning and basting several times.

IF YOU WISH TO MAKE THE PEANUT SAUCE, combine all the ingredients for the sauce in a small pan and cook stirring for about 5 minutes. This sauce will keep for a few days in the fridge. Serve at room temperature in individual small bowls for dipping.

MAKES 4 SATAY STICKS

N

3 chicken breasts, cut into cubes

MARINADE

2 tbsp soy sauce

1 tbsp runny honey

1 tsp mild curry powder

1 tbsp peanut butter

1 small garlic clove, crushed (optional)

PEANUT SAUCE (optional)

3 tbsp peanut butter

125 ml (4 fl oz) coconut milk

1½ tsp brown sugar

1 tsp lemon juice

little ground cayenne pepper (optional)

Teriyaki Chicken Burgers

MAKES 8 BURGERS

❄

1 onion

½ red pepper

1 apple

1 tbsp vegetable oil

350 g (12 oz) chicken breast, roughly chopped, or 350 g (12 oz) minced beef

1 tbsp fresh chopped parsley

½ chicken stock cube

25 g (1 oz) fresh white breadcrumbs

salt and freshly ground black pepper

TERIYAKI SAUCE

3 tbsp soy sauce

½ tbsp sesame oil

3 tbsp sake

3 tbsp mirin

3 tsp caster sugar

Here are tasty burgers that can be cooked on a barbecue or a conventional grill. I have given a recipe for making your own teriyaki sauce, but as a short cut you could use a bought teriyaki sauce. The home-made teriyaki sauce would also make a good marinade for chicken or beef skewers featured on pages 50 and 51.

Finely chop the onion and core, de-seed and chop the red pepper and peel and grate the apple and then squeeze out a little of the juice. Sauté the onion and red pepper in the vegetable oil until softened. Dissolve the stock cube in 45 ml (3 tbsp) boiling water. Then put all the ingredients for the chicken burgers into a food processor, including the onion and red pepper, and chop for a few seconds. Using floured hands, form the mixture into eight burgers.

TO MAKE THE SAUCE, put the ingredients into a small saucepan, bring to the boil, then reduce the heat and simmer for about 2 minutes until slightly thickened and reduced by half. Place the burgers directly on the grill or use a hinged basket, which holds the food between two wire racks. Grill or barbecue for 4 minutes on one side, then baste with the sauce and cook for 1 more minute. Repeat on the other side.

Teriyaki Beef Skewers

MAKES 4 SKEWERS

300 g (10 oz) fillet steak cut
   into cubes

MARINADE
3 tbsp soy sauce
4 tbsp mirin (sweet rice wine)
1 tbsp sesame oil
1 garlic clove, crushed
½ tsp grated fresh ginger root

1 tsp cornflour

A quick, easy and delicious meal is to marinate beef skewers in a tasty combination of flavours and then cook the beef on skewers for 3 to 4 minutes each side. Not only does marinating make the meat really tasty it also makes it much more tender.

Combine all the ingredients for the marinade and marinate the cubes of beef for at least 1 hour. Soak four bamboo skewers in water while the beef is marinating. Before cooking, strain and reserve the marinade and then thread the beef on to the skewers.

COOK THE SKEWERS, either on a barbecue or under a pre-heated grill, for 3 to 4 minutes each side. Meanwhile, mix the cornflour to a paste with 1 tablespoon of the marinade, then pour into a small pan together with the remaining marinade. Bring to the boil and then simmer, stirring until thickened. This will make a delicious dipping sauce.

Annabel's Tasty Chicken Skewers

These skewers can also be interspersed with some vegetables like chunks of red pepper, onion or some button mushrooms. Brush the vegetables with the marinade before cooking the skewers. Alternatively, make skewers with chicken only and serve with boiled rice and stir-fry chopped onion and diced red and yellow peppers in some olive oil and stir into the cooked rice to give it both colour and flavour. This marinade is also good for salmon.

Put the soy sauce and sugar into a small saucepan and gently heat, stirring until the sugar has dissolved. Remove from the heat, stir in the lime juice, vegetable oil, garlic and ginger (if using). Marinate the chicken for at least 1 hour or overnight. Soak eight bamboo skewers in water to prevent them from getting scorched. Pre-heat the oven to 180°C/350°F/Gas 4. Thread the chunks of chicken on to the skewers and cook in the oven for 4 to 5 minutes on each side, basting occasionally with the marinade until cooked through.

MAKES 4 PORTIONS

4 chicken breasts cut into
  chunks

MARINADE

4 tbsp soy sauce

45 g (1½ oz) light muscovado
  sugar

1 tbsp lime or lemon juice

1 tbsp vegetable oil

1 clove garlic, crushed

¼ tsp grated giner (optional)

OVERLEAF: Corn-on-the-cob (p146), Honey and Soy Salmon Skewers (p154)
Annabel's Tasty Chicken Skewers (see above), Strawberries and Peaches with Raspberry Sauce (p155)

Honey and Soy Salmon Skewers

MAKES 4 PORTIONS

350-400 g (12-14 oz) salmon
fillet, skinned and cut into 4
cm (1½ in) cubes

MARINADE
1 tbsp sesame oil
1 tbsp soy sauce
1 tbsp runny honey

This is a really delicious way to cook salmon that keeps the fish really moist and tasty.

Mix together the sesame oil, soy sauce and honey. Marinate the cubes of salmon in this mixture for at least 30 minutes. Meanwhile, soak four bamboo skewers in water to prevent them from getting scorched. Thread the cubes of salmon on to the skewers and barbecue over medium hot coals for about 2 to 3 minutes turning occasionally and basting with the remaining marinade until golden on the outside but still moist and juicy in the centre.

ALTERNATIVELY, pre-heat the grill to medium. Remove the salmon from the marinade, line a baking tray with foil and arrange the cubes of salmon on the tray. Grill for 8 minutes, turning half-way through the cooking time and basting with the remaining marinade.

Strawberries and Peaches with Raspberry Sauce

This is a delicious and quick and easy dessert to make when berry fruits and peaches are in season. The sauce could also be poured over strawberries and blueberries.

If using frozen raspberries, heat them in a saucepan until mushy. If using fresh raspberries, purée them in a food processor. Press the raspberries through a nylon sieve to remove the seeds and stir in the sugar. Halve or quarter the strawberries according to their size and mix with the sliced peaches. Divide the fruit among four serving dishes and pour over the raspberry sauce.

MAKES 4 PORTIONS

250 g (9 oz) raspberries, fresh or frozen
approx. 2 tbsp icing sugar
250 g (9 oz) strawberries
2 ripe peaches, peeled and sliced
4 scoops vanilla ice cream (optional)

Luscious Lychee Lollies

This is a real winner for a hot summer day.

Blend together the lychees with the juice from the can and sieve. Stir in the lemon juice and pour into ice-lolly moulds.

MAKES 4 LARGE OR 6 SMALL ICE LOLLIES

1 x 425 g (14 oz) can lychees
1 tbsp lemon juice

Hallowe'en

You will need: white handkerchiefs, black felt tip pen, lollipops, tissue paper, black ribbon or elastic bands, padded envelopes

Keeping the centre white, write the party details around the edges of the handkerchiefs using the black felt tip pen. Place the centre of the two sheets of tissue paper over the lollipops. Put a handkerchief on top of each and, where the lollipop meets the stick, fasten with the ribbon or use an elastic band. With the black felt tip pen, draw two eyes on to the ghost's face. Send the out invitations to your guests in a padded envelope – decorated with Hallowe'en stickers if you like.

Hallowe'en is a wonderful opportunity to dress up and these are really easy to make. For example, create a ghost from an old white sheet with two holes cut out for eyes and outlined with black felt pen, or make a mummy by wrapping a child in loo paper secured with masking tape. For a witch's costume, use black card for a hat, a black plastic bin bag with the hem cut into zigzags for a dress and add hair made from strips of a green plastic bin bags or use some green wool.

Adding to the Fun

- There are loads of wonderful accessories you can buy at fancy dress shops such as battery-operated headgear with flashing pumpkins or devil's horns; gnarled, luminous witches' fingers or fangs and fake blood.
- If you want children to come trick or treating at your door, carve out a pumpkin and place a lit candle inside.

Hallowe'en Games

Apple Bobbing

Props: large bowl, apples, old newspapers

Half fill a bowl with water and float apples on top. In turn, the children have to lift an apple out of the water using only their teeth while keeping their hands behind their backs. Children can wear aprons if you have them. Spread plenty of newspaper over the floor as this can get quite messy!

Witch's Cauldron

Props: large bowl, cloth to cover bowl, paper, pencils

Suggested contents: hairy toy spider, marshmallow, tea bag, bar of soap, tooth brush, tennis ball, clementine, avocado, emery board, Mars Bar, wine bottle cork.

Place about ten objects in the 'cauldron', turn off the lights and cover it up with a cloth. Let each child in turn feel the contents, leave the room and write down what they are. All the lists are given to an adult who reads out the children's guesses. The one who guesses the most objects correctly is the winner.

Hot Potato Witches

This is a fun way to jolly up a baked potato! If you like, you can remove the flesh from the potato leaving the skin intact, then mash the potato together with some butter, milk and seasoning and stuff it back inside the potato.

Wash and dry the potatoes, prick all over with a fork and brush with oil. Bake in a hot oven for between 1 hour and 1 hour 15 minutes, until tender (alternatively, cook in a microwave/grill combination for about 15 minutes, turning halfway through).

MAKES 2 PORTIONS

2 medium, round baking
   potatoes
a little vegetable oil
2 sheets black paper
1 small bunch of chives
2 stuffed olives
2 baby carrots
1 strip of red pepper
cream cheese, for 'glue'

MAKE LITTLE WITCHES' HATS by cutting circles from the black paper and rolling into a cone. Place the chives in the microwave for 8 to 10 seconds – this will make them more pliable and you will be able to stick them on top of the potato to make the witches' green hair. Decorate the potatoes to look like witches' faces with slices of stuffed olives for the eyes, the tip of a baby carrot for a nose and a strip of red pepper for the mouth. These can be attached to the potato with a dab of cream cheese. Place the black hats on the witches' heads.

Ghoulish Ghost Cakes

Dariole or timbale moulds are the ideal shape for these spooky little cakes.

Pre-heat the oven to 180°C/350°F/Gas 4. Cream together the margarine and sugar with the lemon rind until light and fluffy. Sift together the flour and baking powder. Beat the eggs one at a time with the vanilla essence, adding 1 tablespoon of the flour mixture for each egg. Fold in the remaining flour. Bake in a greased dariole or timbale mould for 20 to 25 minutes.

Turn out the cakes and leave to cool on a wire rack. Take about 100 g (4 oz) icing at a time and roll out thinly on a clean work surface dusted with icing sugar and cut out circles of icing about 18 cm (7 in) diameter. Drape these over the cakes and draw the eyes and noses with black writing icing.

MAKES 10 INDIVIDUAL GHOST CAKES

❄ sponge cake only

100 g (4 oz) soft margarine

100 g (4 oz) caster sugar

1 tsp finely grated lemon rind

100 g (4 oz) self-raising flour

2 eggs

1 tsp pure vanilla essence

450 g (1 lb) white ready-to-roll icing

1 tube black writing icing

Pumpkin Oranges

These oranges are cut to look like mini-pumpkins and then filled with a selection of cut-up fruits or chopped jelly.

Cut a slice from the stalk end of each orange and hollow out using a small sharp knife and teaspoon. Cut out eyes, nose and mouth shapes from the shell and cut a small sliver from the base of the orange so that it stands upright.

Witches' Broomsticks

MAKES 6 BROOMSTICKS

1 packet Twiglets
6 twisted cheese straws
6 chives or strips of spring
   onion

These look very authentic. To make it easier to tie the chives or strips of spring onion, you may need to heat them in a microwave oven for 10 seconds to make them more pliable.

To assemble the broomsticks, attach four Twiglets on to the end of each cheese straw by tying them on with a knotted chive or strip of spring onion.

Dead Man's Fingers

These ghoulish sandwiches look terrific!

Gently flatten the slices of bread with a rolling pin to make them more pliable. Spread with a little margarine and either some cream cheese or peanut butter. Roll up the sandwiches and make three indentations with a blunt knife to form the finger joints. Stick an almond on to each tip with a little cream cheese or peanut butter to form the nails and add some strawberry jam or tomato ketchup for the blood!

N

thin sliced white bread, crusts
removed
soft margarine
cream cheese or peanut butter
almonds
strawberry jam or tomato
ketchup

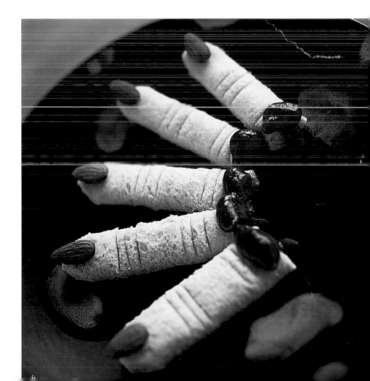

Spider and Bat Cakes

MAKES 10 TO 12 CUPCAKES

🎅 ❄ without decoration

100 g (4 oz) soft margarine

100 g (4 oz) caster sugar

2 eggs

100 g (4 oz) self-raising flour
(substitute 2 tbsp cocoa
powder for 2 tbsp of the
flour for chocolate cakes)

½ tsp orange rind (optional)

SPIDERS

100 g (4 oz) plain or milk
chocolate

liquorice laces

10 chocolate marshmallow tea
cakes

Liquorice Allsorts

mini Smarties

To make five of each design, divide the cake mixture in two and add 1 tablespoon of cocoa powder to half of it.

Pre-heat the oven to 180°C/350°F/Gas 4. Beat together the margarine and sugar until light and fluffy. Beat the eggs into the mixture one at a time, adding a spoonful of the flour with the second egg. Sieve the flour or flour and cocoa mix into the bowl and stir until well blended. If using orange rind add it at this stage to flavour the chocolate sponge mixture.

Line a bun tray with paper cases and spoon into the paper cases until about two-thirds full for the spider cakes. If you want a rounded top for the bats, fill the cases a little more (this mixture will make 12 spider cakes but probably 10 bat cakes). Bake the cakes for 15 to 20 minutes. Put on a wire rack to cool.

SPIDER CAKES Melt the chocolate in a heatproof bowl over a pan of simmering water. Using a palette knife, cover each cake with some of the melted chocolate, arrange six liquorice strips for the spiders' legs and stick a teacake in the centres. Finish with Liquorice Allsorts and Mini Smarties for eyes.

BAT CAKES To make the chocolate frosting, beat the butter until creamy. Sieve together the icing sugar and cocoa and gradually beat into the butter together with the milk using a wooden spoon. When the cakes have cooled, cut off the tops of the cakes and cut into three sections and use the two curved ends to make wings (reserve the middle section).

Draw a V with black writing icing on the wings. Spread a thick layer of chocolate frosting over the surface of the cake, position the wings so that they stand up: you will need to cut small squares of cake from the middle section to position under the wings to prop them up. Stick edible silver balls on top of black liquorice sweets for the bat's eyes.

BATS

100 g (4 oz) softened butter

175 g (6 oz) icing sugar

2 tbsp cocoa powder

1 tbsp milk

1 tube black writing icing

black Liquorice Allsorts

edible silver balls

Bonfire Night

BONFIRE NIGHT INVITATION

You will need: bright coloured shiny card, red foil paper, glue, sticky stars, shiny star confetti (optional)

Cut the shiny card into the shape of a rocket, attach some red foil paper to the end and cut into strips. Decorate the rocket with sticky stars. Put the invitation into an envelope and for fun add a handful of shiny star confetti that will fall out when the envelope is opened.

This party will be held on a winter's evening and the weather will be cold so you will want to prepare some tasty hot food for supper to keep your guests happy. You can also pass around a hot drink like the Spiced Cranberry and Orange Juice given on page 170 and maybe some sausages on sticks while the children are watching the fireworks.

It is a good idea to team up with other parents or friends and pool resources to put on a really good firework display. If you plan to go to a public firework display, you could all meet up either before or afterwards for supper. Fireworks are dangerous so make sure that children are kept well away from them and also warn them never to go near a firework that has been lit but has not gone off. You can, however, give out sparklers to play with, provided they are lit by an adult and that the children are well supervised. Warn them not to touch the sparkler after it has burnt out as it will be very hot and will burn their fingers.

Sticky Drumsticks

A good way to marinate drumsticks is to put the marinade in a clean plastic food or freezer bag, add the drumsticks, twist and seal the top tightly and rub the sauce and chicken together. Then leave the bag in the fridge for at least 1 hour. You can buy Chinese plum sauce in most supermarkets and it adds a delicious flavour to these drumsticks.

Mix together all the ingredients for the marinade. Score the drumsticks three times with a sharp knife. Marinate the drumsticks for at least 1 hour or overnight. Transfer to a baking dish and baste well. Pre-heat the grill to high, then put the chicken under the grill, turn the grill down to medium and cook the drumsticks for about 20 minutes or until cooked through, turning occasionally and basting with the barbecue sauce.

CHECK THE DRUMSTICKS ARE COOKED THROUGH, wrap the ends in aluminium foil and serve with baked beans and baked potatoes. Alternatively, cook the drumsticks in an oven pre-heated to 190°C/375°F/Gas 5 for 35 to 40 minutes.

MAKES 6

6 large drumsticks

MARINADE

2 tsp soy sauce

2 tsp Worcestershire sauce

4 tbsp tomato ketchup

2 tbsp Chinese plum sauce

2 tbsp dark brown sugar

½ tsp Dijon mustard

Catherine Wheel Pizzas

MAKES APPROXIMATELY 12
INDIVIDUAL PINWHEEL PIZZAS

❄

225 g (8 oz) self-raising flour

¼ tsp salt

50 g (2 oz) butter

50 g (2 oz) Cheddar cheese,
grated

1 tsp mixed herbs

150 ml (¼ pint) milk

TOPPING

1 medium onion, chopped

100 g (4 oz) button
mushrooms, chopped

1 tbsp olive oil

2 tbsp red pesto

2 tbsp tomato purée

75 g (3 oz) Cheddar cheese,
grated

These catherine wheel pizzas are just the right size for little fingers. They also make tasty morsels for the grown-ups and look much more attractive than offering slices of pizza at a bonfire party. If you don't want to make your own pastry, make them with frozen shortcrust pastry.

Pre-heat the oven to 180°C/350°F/Gas 4. Sieve together the flour and salt. Using your fingertips, rub in the butter so that it resembles fine breadcrumbs. Stir in the grated cheese and herbs. Stir in the milk until the mixture forms a soft dough. Turn on to a lightly floured surface and knead for 1 minute until smooth (don't knead for too long as the dough becomes greasy).

Roll out the dough on a sheet of non-stick baking paper to a rectangle of about 32 x 20 cm (12 x 8 in). Sauté the onion and mushrooms in the olive oil for 3 to 4 minutes. Stir in the pesto and tomato purée. Spread the mushroom and tomato mixture over the rolled-out dough and sprinkle over the grated cheese.

TO CREATE THE CATHERINE WHEEL EFFECT, use the baking paper as a guide and roll up the dough from the long side. Remove the baking paper and, using a sharp knife, cut into about 12 slices, each about 2 cm (¾ in) thick. Place cut side down on a greased baking tray and bake for about 20 minutes or until golden.

Rocket Kebabs

Raw vegetables are often more appealing to children than cooked, especially when served with a tasty dip.

Mix together the cream cheese, tomato ketchup and milk and stir in the snipped chives.

Thread each of the ingredients on to a skewer ending with a triangle of red pepper so that it looks like a rocket. To make the dip, simply mix together all the ingredients.

MAKES AS MANY AS YOU LIKE

Cheddar cheese
cucumber
celery
carrot
red pepper, cut into triangles

DIP
200 g (7 oz) cream cheese
1 tbsp tomato ketchup
1 tbsp milk
1 tbsp snipped chives

OVERLEAF
Catherine Wheel Pizzas (see left)
Rocket Kebabs (see above)
Sticky Drumsticks (p165)

Warm Spiced Cranberry and Orange Juice

MAKES ABOUT 1 LITRE (2 PINTS)

1 litre (2 pints) cranberry juice
   drink
250 ml (8 fl oz) freshly
   squeezed orange juice
2 cloves
1 cinnamon stick
1 tbsp brown sugar, to taste
a little brandy (optional for
   adults only)

DECORATION
orange, thinly sliced
maraschino cherries

This is a delicious and warming drink to serve while watching the firework display. It is also good cold.

Put the cranberry, orange juice, clove and cinnamon stick, sugar and brandy (if using) in a saucepan and warm gently but do not allow to boil. Remove from the pan, cover and leave for at least 5 minutes to allow the spices to infuse. Strain to remove the clove and cinnamon stick. Gently warm once more and pour into a large jug. Thread a slice of orange and a maraschino cherry on to cocktail sticks to decorate.

Meatballs with Sweet-and-sour Sauce

On a cold winter's night it is nice to give the children a warming supper after watching the fireworks. This recipe is ideal; it is delicious and very popular with my three children and it can be made in advance and frozen if you wish. Serve with rice.

Finely crumble the stock cube and then mix together all the ingredients for the meatballs and chop for a few seconds in a food processor together with 2 tablespoons cold water. Using floured hands, form into about 20 meatballs. Heat the oil in a frying pan and sauté the meatballs, turning occasionally for 10 to 12 minutes until browned.

FOR THE SAUCE, mix together the soy sauce and cornflour. Heat the oil in a pan and sauté the onion for 3 minutes. Add the red pepper and sauté for 2 minutes, stirring occasionally. Add the tomatoes, vinegar and sugar, season with freshly ground black pepper and simmer for 10 minutes. Add the soy sauce mixture and cook for 2 minutes, stirring occasionally. Blend and sieve or put the sauce through a mouli. Pour the sauce over the meatballs, cover and simmer for about 5 minutes.

MAKES 4-5 PORTIONS

❄

MEATBALLS

1 chicken stock cube

450 g (1 lb) lean minced beef

1 onion, finely chopped

1 apple, peeled and grated

50 g (2 oz) white breadcrumbs

1 tbsp chopped fresh parsley

salt and pepper

2 tbsp vegetable oil

1 tbsp soy sauce

½ tbsp cornflour

1 tbsp vegetable oil

1 onion, finely chopped

50 g (2 oz) chopped pepper

1 x 400 g (14 oz) can chopped tomatoes

1 tbsp malt vinegar

1 tsp soft brown sugar

Mini-baked Potatoes

Prick ordinary sized potatoes (not baking potatoes) with a fork. Brush with oil and sprinkle with salt. Bake in an oven pre-heated to 200°C/400°F/Gas 6 for 45 to 55 minutes or until crisp on the outside and tender inside.

MAKES 6 PORTIONS

COCKTAIL SAUCE
1 tbsp tomato ketchup
1½ tbsp mayonnaise
½ tsp Worcestershire sauce
few drops tabasco
pinch celery salt
1 tbsp double cream
salt and white pepper

1 large peeled, stoned and diced avocado
200 g (7 oz) fresh cooked prawns
cucumber slices

There are many simple toppings for baked potatoes like grated cheese and ham, baked beans or flaked tuna, spring onion, sweetcorn and mayonnaise. However, for something a little different try the three ideas given here.

Avocado and Prawn Cocktail Topping

Mix together all the ingredients to make the cocktail sauce. Then combine the avocado and prawns and mix thoroughly with the sauce. Cut a cross in the top of the baked potato, spoon in the topping and decorate with a cucumber slice on a cocktail stick to form a sail.

Mexican Chicken Topping

Mix the chicken with the chilli powder, oregano, 7.5 ml (½ tbsp) of the olive oil and some salt and pepper. Heat the remaining oil in a pan and sauté the onion for 1 minute until beginning to soften. Add the chicken and sauté for about 4 minutes until cooked through. Stir in the chopped tomato. Cut a cross in the baked potatoes, spoon over the topping and decorate each one with a tortilla chip sail.

SERVES 4

1 chicken breast, diced small

generous pinch of mild chilli
    powder

¼ tsp dried oregano

1 tbsp oil

salt and freshly ground pepper

½ small onion, chopped

1 ripe tomato, diced

tortilla chips

Salsa and Gruyère Cheese Topping

Sauté the onion, garlic and red pepper in the oil for 4 minutes. Add the tomatoes, parsley, tabasco and salt and pepper and simmer for 10 minutes. Cut the Gruyère cheese into six triangles. Cut a cross in the baked potatoes, spoon over the topping and dollop a tablespoon of sour cream on top. Decorate each potato with a cheese triangle for a sail.

SERVES 6

½ small onion, chopped

½ clove crushed garlic

½ small red pepper, chopped

½ tbsp vegetable oil

1 x 200 g (7 oz) can chopped
    tomatoes

½ tbsp chopped fresh parsley

few drops tabasco

salt and black pepper

6 tbsp sour cream

Gruyère cheese

Toffee Apples

MAKES 8 TO 10 TOFFEE APPLES

TOFFEE COATING

450 g (1 lb) demerara sugar

50 g (2 oz) butter

2 tsp vinegar

1 tbsp golden syrup

150 ml (¼ pint) water

8 to 10 small apples, washed
   and dried

Toffee apples always remind me of going to the fair and they are ideal for children to eat while they are watching a firework display. They are easy to make but for best results you should use a sugar thermometer – these are cheap to buy and can be found in any cookware store.

Put all the ingredients for the toffee coating into a heavy-based saucepan. Heat gently, stirring all the time, until the sugar has dissolved. Bring to the boil and boil rapidly without stirring until the temperature reaches 143°C/290°F on a sugar thermometer. If you don't have a thermometer, drop a little of the hot syrup into cold water – the coating is ready when it separates into hard threads.

BEFORE COVERING THE APPLES, push thick wooden skewers, lolly sticks or even wooden chopsticks into them. Dip them carefully into the hot toffee mixture, swirling them around and allowing the excess to drip off so that the coating is not too thick. Leave to set on wax paper or greased aluminium foil.

Strawberry and Rhubarb Crumble

This is one of my favourite crumbles. It is a delicious combination of flavours and the pink colour of the rhubarb looks so attractive. It is also very quick and easy to prepare. Serve with custard or ice cream.

Pre-heat the oven to 200°C/400°F/Gas 6. To make the topping, mix the flour together with a pinch of salt in a bowl and rub in the butter using your fingertips until the mixture resembles breadcrumbs. Stir in the demerara sugar and ground almonds.

Cut the rhubarb into small pieces and halve the strawberries. Put them into a suitable ovenproof dish (a round Pyrex dish looks good), sprinkle over the sugar and mix with the fruit.

Cover the fruit with the crumble topping and sprinkle over a tablespoon of water (this will help to make the topping crispy). Bake in the oven for about 25 minutes.

MAKES 5 PORTIONS

❄ **N**

CRUMBLE TOPPING

150 g (5 oz) plain flour

generous pinch of salt

100 g (4 oz) cold butter, cut into pieces

75 g (3 oz) demerara sugar

50 g (2 oz) ground almonds

400 g (14 oz) rhubarb

100 g (4 oz) strawberries

4 tbsp caster sugar

Christmas

CHRISTMAS CRACKER INVITATION
You will need: toilet roll holders, white paper, shiny red paper, gold ribbon, Christmas decorations like holly
Write the details of the party on a piece of paper and wrap it around an empty toilet roll holder. If you wish, put a little gift like a balloon or sweet inside the toilet roll. Cover with gold tissue and shiny red paper and tie the ends to look like a cracker with gold ribbon. If you like, stick on some Christmas decorations like holly. Send out in a padded envelope.

Christmas is a magical time of year and when the theme for a party is Christmas, it is a fantastic excuse for dressing up. Children will love to dress up like such perennial favourites as Father Christmas, angels, snowmen, Christmas trees – or even Rudolph the red-nosed reindeer.

Adding to the Fun

• Get the children involved in activities like baking and decorating Christmas cookies. You can use the recipe for Stained Glass Window Biscuits (page 180) or Heart-shaped Faces (page 64) and use Christmas cookie cutters like bells, angels, stockings and Christmas trees to shape the biscuits. Put out plenty of decorating items like coloured sugar, tubes of writing icing and sprinkles.

• It is also fun to make snowflakes from pieces of paper folded into quarters. You will need lots of pairs of scissors, pencils, crayons and glitter. Show the children how to draw patterns on the folded paper, which are then cut out so that when the paper is opened up the result is a cut-out snowflake ready for colouring in decorating with glitter before hanging on the tree.

- Every year we sing Christmas songs and carols but how well do we know them? You could play excerpts of various Christmas music and ask the children to try to write down the titles of the songs. The child with the most correct answers is the winner.

Christmas Games

Hunt the Christmas Card
Props: old Christmas cards, scissors
Cut old Christmas cards in half. Put one set of the halves in a basket and divide them among the children. Hide the other halves around the house and ask the children to search for as many of them as possible in a given time.

Christmas Stocking
Props: Christmas stocking, various objects
Put various objects into a Christmas stocking without the children seeing what they are. Have a mixture of things, some more unusual than others. The children then have to feel the stocking and guess what is inside.

Pin the Nose on Rudolph
Props: blindfold, large picture of Rudolph, red nose and drawing pin
This is a Christmas version of pin the tail on the donkey. Every child has a go trying to pin the red nose in the correct place while blindfolded. It is a good idea to turn the children around a few times once they are blindfold to disorientate them. Mark the spot where each child places the drawing pin with a cross and their initials to see who comes the closest.

Christmas Drawings
Props: paper and pencils
Make a list of things to do with Christmas, such as reindeers, snowmen, Christmas puddings. Divide the children into teams and ask the first child from each team to come up so you can whisper in their ear the name of the object. They must then go back to their team members and draw it. As soon as a team member guesses correctly, the next person goes up, and so on. To make this more difficult, ask the children to draw the object with the wrong hand.

Christmas Cake

N

350 g (12 oz) raisins

275 g (10 oz) sultanas

275 g (10 oz) currants

4 tbsp each brandy and port

250 g (9 oz) butter, softened

250 g (9 oz) dark muscovado sugar

350 g (12 oz) plain flour

1 tsp baking powder

pinch of salt

6 eggs

50 g (2 oz) ground almonds

1 tsp mixed spice

1 tsp cinnamon

1 tsp grated lemon rind

50 g (2 oz) mixed peel

100 g (4 oz) glacé cherries, halved

100 g (4 oz) pecans, chopped

125 g (41/2 oz) apricot jam

2-3 tbsp water

extra glacé fruits and pecans

This cake matures if kept so I make mine three to four weeks before Christmas.

Put the raisins, sultanas and currants in a large bowl and pour in the brandy and port. Leave to soak overnight. Next day, line and grease a 23 cm (9 in) diameter cake tin. Tie a double thickness of brown paper around the outside to come about 4 cm (1½ in) higher than the cake. Pre-heat the oven to 150°C/300°F/Gas 2.

BEAT THE BUTTER AND SUGAR TOGETHER until fluffy. Sift the flour, baking powder and salt. Beat in the eggs one at a time adding some of the flour mixture with each. Beat in the remaining flour and almonds. Add mixed spice, cinnamon and lemon rind. Finally mix in dried fruits and nuts. Spoon into the tin and level. Bake in the centre of the oven for 2½ hours (after 1 hour, cover the cake with greaseproof paper), or until the cake is firm to the touch and a skewer in the centre comes out clean. Leave to cool in the tin for about 30 minutes. Turn out on to a wire rack and cool and then wrap in aluminium foil and store.

TO DECORATE, warm the jam and water in a saucepan. Sieve and brush some over the cake. Arrange the glacé fruits and nuts and brush on more of the glaze. Finally, tie a ribbon around the cake.

Stained-glass Window Biscuits

MAKES 25 TO 30 BISCUITS

100 g (4oz) butter

50 g (2 oz) caster sugar

175 g (6 oz) plain flour

2 tbsp cornflour

pinch of salt

1 tsp milk

18 clear boiled sweets, in
   assorted colours

DECORATIONS

125 g (5 oz) ready-to-roll
   white icing

red and blue edible paste food
   colouring

royal icing (see page 62)

edible silver balls

These novelty Christmas cookies shaped like Christmas trees, stars, bells and snowmen are fun to make together with children and look very attractive hanging on a Christmas tree.

Pre-heat the oven to 180°C/350°F/Gas 4. Cream together the butter and sugar. Sift in the flours together with a pinch of salt and mix together with the creamed butter and sugar. Add the milk and knead to form a soft ball of dough.

With one colour at a time and using a rolling pin, crush the sweets in their wrappers. Sprinkle flour on a clean work surface and roll out the dough to a thickness of about 5 mm (¼ in). Using a selection of Christmas cookie cutters, cut out shapes and arrange on baking sheets lined with parchment. Cut out a triangle or circle in the centre of each biscuit, making sure you leave a good edge at the top and around the sides.

COMPLETELY FILL EACH TRIANGLE OR CIRCLE with crushed boiled sweets of one colour. Make a hole at the top of each biscuit using a drinking straw so that you will be able to thread a ribbon through it later. Bake for 10 to 12 minutes until golden. While

the biscuits are still warm, check the holes are still there, otherwise gently push a straw through again. Do not remove the biscuits from the baking tray until they have cooled as the boiled sweets need to harden. But once set, gently lift the biscuits off the paper with a palette knife and cool on a wire rack.

Roll out some of the ready-to-roll icing and colour some red and some blue for the Father Christmas hat and the snowman's scarf. Decorate the biscuits with coloured rolled-out icing, piped royal icing and edible silver balls for eyes. Thread ribbon through the holes to make loops for hanging.

ice-cream Snowballs

Simply roll scoops of ice cream in grated white chocolate and return to the freezer to set.

OVERLEAF
Baby Christmas Puddings (p184)
Mini-Christmas Presents (p185)
Christmas Fairy Cakes (p186)

Baby Christmas Puddings

MAKES ABOUT 20

200 g (7 oz) plain chocolate

50 g (2 oz) butter

2 tbsp golden syrup

225 g (8 oz) digestive biscuits

50 g (2 oz) dried apricots, finely chopped

50 g (2 oz) golden sultanas

50 g (2 oz) raisins

50 g (2 oz) glacé cherries, chopped

75 g (3 oz) ready-to-roll white icing

icing sugar for dusting

1 tbsp apricot jam

50 g (2 oz) green ready-to-roll icing

edible sugar-coated red balls or use 25 g (1 oz) ready-to-roll red icing

Children like the look of Christmas puddings but often don't like the taste. These miniature Christmas puddings look fantastic and children love eating them too!

Melt the chocolate together with the butter and golden syrup in a saucepan over a low heat, stirring occasionally for about 4 minutes. Put the biscuits into a plastic bag and crush into very small pieces with a rolling pin. Mix the biscuits into the melted chocolate mixture together with the dried fruit and glacé cherries. Set aside to cool in the fridge for about 30 minutes.

TO MAKE THE PUDDINGS, use your hands to roll tablespoons of the mixture into about 20 balls. Dust a work surface with icing sugar and roll out the white icing until quite thin. Use a small petal shape cutter or a sharp knife to cut circular wavy shapes from the icing. Brush the tops of the puddings with warmed apricot jam and stick the icing circles on top. Roll out the green icing until quite thin and cut out holly leaves using a small cutter. If you can't find ready-made green icing, you can make your own by kneading white icing with a few drops of green food colouring. Use tiny red sugar-coated balls for the berries or make from a small quantity of red icing. Attach to the puddings with apricot jam.

Mini-Christmas Presents

You can have fun decorating each one of these a little differently. You can use the hollow top of a pen to cut out circles to make spots.

Pre-heat the oven to 180°C/350°F/Gas 4. Grease and line a 30 x 23 cm (12 x 9 in) cake tin. Cream together the butter and sugar. Sieve the almonds and the flour and add to the mixture. Beat the eggs lightly and add gradually to the mixture together with the milk and almond essence. Spoon the mixture into the tin, level the surface and bake for about 30 minutes. Leave to cool in the tin, then turn out on to a wire rack. Cut into 5 cm (2 in) squares. If you want taller parcels, sandwich two squares together with some jam in between.

FOR THE ICING, take one quarter of the icing and colour it red. Roll out the icing on a work surface dusted with icing sugar until quite thin and cover the top and sides of each cake with icing, folding the edges over to form a parcel. You can also cut strips of white and red rolled icing to make a striped parcel. Decorate with icing cut into shapes with small novelty cutters or mini-sweets and finish off by using strips of liquorice for ribbons around the presents.

MAKES 9 MINI-CHRISTMAS PRESENTS

N ❄ without decoration

225 g (8 oz) butter

225 g (8 oz) caster sugar

100 g (4 oz) ground almonds

185 g (6½ oz) self-raising flour, sifted

4 eggs

4 tbsp milk

1½ tsp almond essence

strawberry or raspberry jam (optional)

500 g (1 lb 2 oz) ready-to-roll white icing

red food paste colouring

mini-sweets

red, green and black liquorice laces

Christmas Fairy Cakes

MAKES 12 CAKES

❄ without decoration

100 g (4 oz) soft margarine

100 g (4 oz) caster sugar

2 eggs

100 g (4 oz) self-raising flour

1 tsp pure vanilla essence

CHOCOLATE BUTTERCREAM

100 g (4 oz) unsalted butter
  (room temperature)

150 g (6 oz) icing sugar,
  sieved

50 g (2 oz) plain chocolate,
  melted

It's fun to turn fairy cakes into special Christmas treats by decorating them with a Christmas theme.

Pre-heat the oven to 180°C/350°F/Gas 4. Cream the margarine and sugar together until light and fluffy and then beat in the eggs one at a time together with 1 tablespoon of the flour. Add the vanilla and fold in the remaining flour. Line a bun tin with paper cases and half fill each case with the mixture. Bake in an oven for about 20 minutes. Remove and put on a wire rack to cool before decorating.

Christmas Puddings

To make the chocolate buttercream, beat the butter until softened and gradually beat in the icing sugar, then beat in the cooled melted chocolate. Spread the chocolate buttercream over four of the fairy cakes. Roll out some of the ready-to-roll icing and cut out shapes to form the brandy butter topping on the Christmas puddings. Colour a little of the ready-to-roll icing green and cut out holly shapes, which can be decorated with red candy balls.

Robin Red Breasts

Colour some of the ready-to-roll icing red and some brown. Roll out the red icing into circles large enough to cover the fairy cakes. Spread a little of the chocolate buttercream on the tops of the cakes and place the circles of red icing on top. Cut out shapes from the brown icing to form the robin's face and attach the strips of chocolate flake with some of the buttercream icing to form the tail. Add edible silver balls for eyes.

Father Christmas

Roll out some of the white icing and cut out circles to fit the fairy cakes. Attach these to the cakes with a little of the chocolate buttercream. Colour some of the icing red and cut out triangles to form hats. To make royal icing for piping, beat in enough egg white to the icing sugar bit by bit to get a good consistency and use to pipe across the hats and to make beards. Decorate with edible silver balls and liquorice or chocolate chips for eyes.

DECORATION
750 g (1 lb 10 oz) ready-to-roll icing
green, red and brown food colouring pastes
2 chocolate flakes
edible silver balls
edible red candy balls
black liquorice
chocolate chips

ROYAL ICING
(see page 62)

index

ACKNOWLEDGEMENTS

To Nicholas, Lara and Scarlett who have been
enthusiastic guinea pigs to my triumphs and disasters,
may life always be one big party.

To my mother Evelyn Etkind in appreciation
of all the parties she gave for me.

To my husband Simon Karmel for whom
happiness is a bowl of jelly.

To Daniel Pangbourne who has brought my
food alive with his superb photography.

I would also like to thank Sara Lewis, Jo Pratt,
Amelia Thorpe, Joanna Carreras, Martin Lovelock,
Emma Callery, Tessa Evelegh, David Karmel, Jacqui Morley,
Marina Magpoc, Jane Hamilton and Letty Catada.

The publishers would like to thank Simon Brown for permission
to use the photographs on pages 9 and 157 and Annabel Karmel
for permission to use the photographs on pages 29, 42, 47, 48,
54, 55, 65, 70, 73, 80, 91, 105, 124, 129, 131, 143, 158, 160,
161 and 179.

PARTY GOODS SPECIALISTS

A Piece of Cake
Telephone: 01844 213428
(food colour pens, paste
colour, etc.)

Letterbox
Telephone: 01872 580885
(original party toys)

Oscar's Den
Telephone: 020 7328 6683
www.oscarsden.com
(party equipment)

Party Directory
Telephone: 01276 850501

Party Pieces
Telephone: 01635 201844

Partyworks
0870 240 2103
www.partybypost.co.uk

Squire's Kitchen
Telephone: 01252 711749
(cake equipment specialists)

Also by Annabel Karmel
Published by Ebury Press

The New Complete
Baby and Toddler
Meal Planner
ISBN: 0 09 186360 0
£10.99

Annabel Karmel's
Small Helpings
ISBN: 0 09 186373 2
£10.99

Annabel Karmel's
Quick Children's Meals
ISBN: 0 09 185189 0
£10.99

Annabel Karmel's New
Baby and Toddler Cookbook
ISBN: 0 09 182558 X
£10.99

Annabel Karmel's
Family Meal Planner
ISBN: 0 09 186795 9
£14.99

All are available from good bookshops
or simply call TBS Direct on 01206 255800